ᵀᴴᴱ**ERGONOMIC** COUPLE

a brief guide

to creating a better fit

in your relationship

Barbara Wetzel

THE **ERGONOMIC** COUPLE

a brief guide

to creating a better fit

in your relationship

Practical information you can start using today

Barbara Wetzel

Barbara Wetzel
1507 Buttonwood Dr.
Fort Collins, CO 80525
(970)449-9128
barbarawetzel@theergonomiccouple.com

Disclaimer

The author and publisher endeavor to make the information in this book accurate and up to date. It is a general guide. Before taking action on significant medical, legal or financial matters you should consult with qualified professionals who can help you consider your unique circumstances. The author and publisher cannot accordingly accept any liability for any loss or damage suffered as a consequence of relying on the information contained in this book.

Mention of specific leaders in research, education, marriage and family therapy, or other authorities in this book does not imply they endorse this book. Internet addresses are accurate at the time of printing.

Feelings list by Marshall Rosenberg and The Center for Non-Violent Communication in Appendix A reprinted by permission.

IBSN: 978-0-615-37061-3

Library of Congress Control Number: 2010912982

Cover design and interior page layout by Kerrie Lian, under contract with MacGraphics Services: http://www.MacGraphics.net

The Ergonomic Couple: A Brief Guide to Creating a Better Fit in Your Relationship/ Barbara Wetzel

Includes bibliographical references.

1. Couple's enrichment. 2. Marriage enrichment. 3. Couple's communication.

G H Goldstein Press

ACKNOWLEDGMENTS

My mother, Lois Wetzel; my aunt, Margaret Hoskey, my maternal grandparents George and Margaret Goldstein; sisters, Cathy Commons, Lois Wetzel, and Janine Donzelli; Uncle Pete Hoskey and his wife Mary; cousin Christopher Hoskey; niece Michele Wetzel; nephews Mitchell and Ken. And my in-laws Don and Janet Wells, Laura Killian, Jessica Wells and Brooke Jacobsen, Peter Wells and Jennifer Elpers, and Julie, Paul and Geoff DeSena.

Friends and colleagues Cyndi Dodds and Steve Buff, Jill and Tom Vosburg, Ron and Inge Wykstra, Sarah Gabbay and Sue Mohr, Char deSerte-Gilliland, Toni Zimmerman, Shelly Haddock, Jennifer Matheson, Rita Dykstra, Brook Bretthauer, Debra Wallace, Lia Softis-Nall, Ray and Shirley Yang, Atsuko Okazawa, Bobbie Beach, Carol Pfaffly, Christina Gomez, Colleen Sterry, Damond Dotson, Andrea Holt, Dave Braham, Elaine Purdum, Diego Vega, Jen Aberle, Jen Krafchick, Jennifer Moné, Joan Cmar, Katie Godfrey, Kelly Walker-Haley, Kris Ullstrup, Mark Adams, Lori Lund, Joanna Pepin, Maria Tomson, Mark Cummings, Mary Mills, Mia Towbin, Maura Dunn, Michael Eade, Michelle Scheetz, Erik Sween, Mike Ruttenberg, Lisa Rust, Nat Kees, Kevin Oltjenbruns, Alicia Cook, Osnat Arbel, Rhonda Parmley, Sondra Medina, Stephanie Seng, Veronica Rivera, Antoniette Gupta, Catherine and Larry Watson, Lin Wilder, John Grogan, John Morse, Barbara Fisher, Bob Calhoun, Marilyn MacIntyre, Lisa Pendleton, Barbara Stutsman, Denis Lane, Kevin Lyness, Andrea Faudel, Jaque Martin, David MacPhee, Jean McBride, Joael Arnaudo, Sharon Korman, Christine Basset, Leah Hughes, John Gray, Sarah Carlson, Hanna Vaughn, April Malcolm, Rod Mayes, Fred Rees, Jim Wahler, Kandi Moore, Barbara Cohen, Martha Goodell, Karen Searock, Katy Doherty, Kathy Cook, Dakota Marin, Scarlett Hillis, Beth Syder, Karen Reddick, Karen Saunders and Kerrie Lian of MacGraphics Services, Mike and Deb Hooker.

The resilient and resourceful people with whom I have had the privilege to work with over the years.

My Cozumel friends Ann Ruhlman, Janice VanderBok, Audrey Ellard, Vivian Olmsted, Ken and Catherine White, Sally Hurwitch, and Beatriz Cornejo.

My "Sanity and a Breath" resources for humor, perspective, pure entertainment, information and stimulation: National Public Radio, specifically KUNC of Northern Colorado, The Daily Show, The Colbert Report and The Rachel Maddow Show.

And the love, support, inspiration, and collaboration of my partner and lover of 32 years, Christopher Wells, and our son, Whitney Wells, and daughter, Sydney Wells. And my four-legged family members Emily, Jamaica, Tigre, Aurora, Zoë, Miikka, Wallace and Tomasa.

To **life** . . .

You are probably familiar with the concept of ergonomics in the workplace, whether you work on mechanics, housework, at a desk, in a truck, or on your feet. There is a common awareness of what positions and motions are best for your ongoing optimal functioning.

How do you avoid hurting yourself? How do you learn about the optimum comfort in your circumstances? How do you avoid unnecessary stress or harm? How do you avoid repetitive pattern injury? How do you replace bad/harmful/unhealthy habits with new habits that are beneficial to you, your partner, and your relationship?

This book uses an ergonomic view to explain how to improve the fit in your couples relationship.

er•go•nom•ic, *adjective*

Intended to provide optimum comfort and to avoid stress or injury.

Ergonomics is designing relationships for optimizing human well-being and overall system performance.

In this couples reference book, I provide guidelines and examples of how couples systems can benefit from basic pattern changes based on these ergonomic principles.

1. **Safety**

   What you do should not harm you or your partner. However, with change and growth there is the challenge of the unfamiliar, being vulnerable, and having to do productive work.

2. **Comfort**

   What you do needs to reduce stress in a healthy way. It may still be difficult and unfamiliar.

3. **Ease of use**

   What you do needs to be a realistic step you can take today, now.

4. **Performance**

   What you do needs to improve your quality of life on a meaningful level for you and your partner.

5. **Aesthetics**

   What you do should move you toward a sense of balance and harmony in your life.

Throughout this book, I alternate the use of gender pronouns. All examples are interchangeable for both genders.

In cases where the research on heterosexual couples points to gender patterns, I use the most common gender pattern references in my writing. This may parallel your couple experience or it may not.

Occasionally, I use same-gender pronouns because I recognize and include same-sex couples in my work.

Please keep in mind, the patterns in your relationship are unique, even when there are many similarities to the general examples I give. Take the parts of this book that are helpful to you and leave the rest.

TABLE OF CONTENTS

Framing Book Chapters 1, 2, 3

- Is this book for you?
- How to use this book.

Stages of Change Chapter 5

- It is effective to match behavioral goals with readiness level

Six Relationship Dimensions Chapters 4 and 6-17

- Communication
- Conflict
- Balance
- Play
- Intimacy
- Finances

Personal Relationship Guide and Tool Box Chapters18 and 19

- Create together
- Put it in writing or an equivalent reliable format for future consultation.
- Update as needed.

Good judgment comes from experience which comes from poor judgment.

—unknown

CHAPTER 1

WHY THIS BOOK?

Being a couple requires work, regardless of the type of relationship you have. There are three main types of relationships:

- A warm, loving, respectful relationship
- A "going through the motions, dead on the vine" relationship
- An ongoing hot and cold war of power struggles relationship

Most of us can relate to some of each of these relationship types. What's important is what percentage of time is spent in each mode? How would you primarily define your relationship?

It takes more energy to maintain a "dead" or "battling" relationship than it does to maintain a passionate loving relationship. This ergonomic approach to improve the fit in your relationship may initially take extra energy to change unwanted patterns. It is an investment in a system that will work more optimally in the long run.

A "good" coupleship is committed to a journey of personal growth, skill development, and perseverance *with a witness* who has seen and experienced your faults and mistakes; a witness who is privy to your hopes and dreams as well as your struggles, fears, and hurts. Healthy coupleship is a character building experience and a journey of self-discovery that can include many romantic and blissful moments.

In this book, I present practical information, tools, and skills for improving your fit as a couple that can be used in a matter of minutes, whether you are a new couple or have been together twenty years.

Your challenge is to take fifteen minutes twice a week to learn a new skill or upgrade an old one, and commit to practicing the desired behaviors until they are a habit. Practice, feedback, and more practice are the keys, once you have the tools.

My philosophy is that not only
are you responsible for your life,
but doing the best at this moment puts you in the best place
for the next moment.

—Oprah Winfrey

CHAPTER 2

IS THIS BOOK FOR YOU?

This resource book is for couples who enjoy their relationship and seek practical tools to improve fit and functioning and to develop a method for achieving their personal ergonomic fit. It is for couples in which both partners want to make the effort to grow and renew their relationship and who don't define their relationship primarily in problem terms. It is possible to grow the pleasures and playfulness in a relationship if both partners make the effort to learn and uniquely apply the skills outlined in this book.

There are relationship issues that require professional help. This book doesn't address the following couples' issues:

- Multiple affairs
- Addiction to substances such as alcohol, recreational, or prescription drugs
- Abusive behavior or language (see Appendix C)
- Chronic lying

You and your partner can't get very far together as a couple until these obvious and significant individual patterns are changed. This includes addressing—individually and as a couple—the underlying emotional issue(s) or trauma(s) that likely predate the negative behavior patterns.

If your partner has an uncanny history of not changing his behaviors, I predict that he is more likely to continue in the same undesirable pattern. If this is the case, your primary goal is to change the undesirable patterns in yourself and how you interact with your partner. Your partner will have to adjust to the new you. From his reactions and responses, you can thoughtfully shape more desirable patterns for yourself.

It is preferable to work on goals together as a couple. If you are the only one who wants to work on your relationship at this time, I recommend you read this book and consult with a Marriage and Family Therapist (someone who is a member in good standing in the American Association for Marriage and Family Therapy at AAMFT.org).

Everything that happens to
us during our lives causes a
necessary reaction in our
central nervous system ...
If we live a restricted, narrow
life, our brain adapts to it.
If we suffer years of anxiety,
fear and despair, our brain
adapts to it. On the other hand,
if we enjoy years of contentment,
confidence and hope, our brain
adapts to that. And with very
different effects.

—Thomas Hanna

CHAPTER 3

HOW TO USE THIS BOOK

The design of this resource book fits into a busy life. Worksheets are included to help you establish where you are on a specific dimension in your couple relationship such as communication, play, finance, or sexuality and to make a blueprint of how you would like your relationship to grow in that area. You may fill them out in detail, use them for discussions, or just peruse them for ideas.

I've written this book with a number of different learning styles in mind. There are worksheets for the more detailed verbal processors, bolding for the processors who need fewer words (especially initially), analogies for memory aids, and experiential exercises for practicing. Not all of it fits one person's processing style. Use it in the manner that works best for you individually and as a couple.

Just like building a business, house, or career, there is both a science and an art to relationships. This book shares some of the nuts and bolts of couple relationships in plain English. It informs you of basic relationship tools, how to use them, and how to keep using them. With practice, it will empower the relationship artists in you and your partner to design the flexible organic structure of your relationship.

When I work with couples and they ask me, "How should our relationship be?" I respond, "How would you like it to be?" There is well-documented research on how to get your relationship where you want it to be. Additionally, there are many myths and misconceptions about relationships that contribute to unrealistic relationship expectations, and to the high divorce rate.

There is solid research on many aspects of couple relationships. These include communication, power, intimacy, sexuality, gender, roles, chores, language, brain chemistry, anger management, self-esteem, finance, happiness, purposefulness, flow, and a myriad of other aspects, which are all threads in the colorful canvas of couple relationships. Knowledge in the different aspects of couple relationships is always growing. How these different areas unfold in your relationship is unique.

Assuming that you will meet someone, fall in love, and have a healthy, loving relationship *without work and awareness*, is like assuming you can build a house because you want one and you grew up in one.

Whether you are in a new relationship or have been together for 20 years, *there are areas in your relationship where you can improve the fit and things you can learn.* In long-term relationships, growing the different dimensions of your coupleness is invigorating and renewing.

To improve the ergonomic fit in your couple relationship, use the "Which Stage of Relationship Growth Are You In?" Form, as needed, to determine where you and your partner are, as you read about a particular relationship dimension. Use each other's feedback for any dimension to establish a plan of growth, enrichment, or renewal. Put your plan into action. Write down goals and agreements. Take time for feedback and assessment of your goals.

Take the time to cherish and celebrate your growth. As unromantic as it sounds, schedule time to spend together reviewing and renewing your relationship. It takes practice to discover what love and romance are built on.

Use this book to create your personal guide for how you would like your couple relationship to feel and to function. This way you and your partner have more than a general idea of what a healthy, loving relationship looks like and feels like for each of you. Bear in mind it is unlikely that you will have identical views. There will be conversations, negotiations, compromises, and more negotiations. Some conversations will be easier than others.

I wish you a good journey.

CHAPTER 4

RELATIONSHIP DIMENSIONS

A journey of 1,000 miles begins with a single step.

~ Lao-tzu

The couple relationship dimensions in this book are:

- Communication
- Conflict
- Balance: Individual, Couple, and Family
- Play
- Emotional and Physical Intimacy
- Financial Management

It is unrealistic to expect to work on all of these dimensions effectively at one time. Pick no more than two areas to work on at a time.

For the more challenging dimensions or parts of dimensions, focus on each one for approximately three months. (This is assuming a thoughtful plan with regular feedback and adjustments.) You will see change, growth, and benefits right away. However, *the key is repetition until the change becomes a lifestyle.*

Examining your relationship for optimum ergonomic fit is not a one-time event; it is a recurring process to be practiced again and again.

Take a minimum of fifteen minutes, twice a week (most weeks) to talk about, brainstorm, or work on any dimension of your coupleship.

Improvements in one dimension of your relationship tend to positively impact all the dimensions and the whole relationship, just as neglect in one area tends to negatively impact the whole system.

The first step will be to prioritize what dimensions you want to nurture first.

Here is a fifteen minute exercise to help you decide where to focus. *Notice what is working well first.* Each of you, individually, list the three dimensions in your relationship where you feel you are on the right track, or the dimensions with which you have the fewest issues.

Next, list the two or three dimensions or parts of dimensions you each struggle with or find challenging.

If there is any overlap in your challenging lists, start work there.

In the event that there is no overlap, then you can do an odd-even exercise. On odd weeks of the month (first and third), work on one dimension of the relationship and on even weeks (second and fourth), work on the other. If there are leftover days of the month, you can decide to work on both or neither for those few days.

Coupleness is a dance, a conversation, an art form to be lived every day.

Ric Masten, a troubadour and traveling Unitarian minister, wrote many poems and songs about couples. One of my favorites is, *Let It Be a Dance,* the chorus is:

Let it be a dance we do,
May I have this dance with you?
Through the good times and the bad times, too,
Let it be a dance.

CHAPTER 5

WHICH STAGE OF RELATIONSHIP GROWTH ARE YOU IN?

You may be in different stages of growth in different areas of your relationship. The different areas are all related and growth in one area frequently invites growth in others. It is ergonomic to know what stage you are in in any given area.

All of us can relate to struggles with change and growth. *Be verbally and emotionally respectful with each other in all aspects of this process.* You and your partner will certainly have different levels of readiness in the various and overlapping areas of your relationship. *There is no need to make these differences into a power struggle.* Diversity of experiences and diversity of thoughts in the individuals in any couple is the norm, and there are more similarities than differences.

NOTICE where each of you are in the process.

ACKNOWLEDGE where you are.

ACCEPT this is where you are starting from today.

The first step to making significant change is acknowledging where you are, so you can take the appropriate next step. One stage is not better than another; they are all part of the growth process. Each stage lays a foundation for the next stage. This framework is a map for addressing mindful growth. It is based on the Transtheoretical Model by James O. Prochaska. (See more information on his model at http://www.prochange.com/ttm.) This process is divided into six stages as follows:

1. Undeveloped Awareness
2. Developing Awareness
3. Planning Application of Awareness, Planning Action
4. Taking Thoughtful Action
5. Using Thoughtful Feedback
6. Maintenance Plan

1. UNDEVELOPED AWARENESS

A person in this stage is not aware of the need for growth in a particular relationship dimension or the intrinsic rewards of growth. He often feels the situation is fine as it is. He does not know that there can be something better. Perhaps he has paid lip service to the idea of change; however, he is unaware that he can research, develop, and apply a plan for growth. He may use denial to keep from moving forward.

STRATEGIES

Expose someone with undeveloped awareness to relationship information in everyday settings. Read an article aloud from a newspaper, magazine, or the Internet. Leave a relationship book lying around with a catchy title, such as *Empowering Couples: Building on Your Strengths*, by Olson and Olson, or *The Ergonomic Couple: A Brief Guide to Improving the Fit in Your Relationship*. Watch stand-up comics and movies where relationship issues are the topic. Watch the dynamic presentations on TED.com that are free, educational, inspirational, and entertaining.

The best time to approach any reoccurring problematic issue is not when it is occurring. In other words, don't talk to someone in the morning about being grumpy in the morning. Rather, do this at a time of low stress and high communication. Bring up the idea of attending a lecture or reading a couple of pages from a book on relationships, communication, or sex (whichever topic is least threatening to both of you) and set a date to discuss it. Oftentimes, an unaware person moves suddenly to a different stage when he is reacting to a crisis, sudden change, loss, or threat of loss. And, far too often, he reverts to old patterns once the crisis has passed.

2. DEVELOPING AWARENESS

A person with developing awareness realizes that the relationship needs attention. She's willing to think about it and even articulate her dissatisfaction about the status quo. Often, a person with developing awareness has a whole bookshelf full of partially read self-help books. Because you're reading this self-help book now, there is a good chance you can relate to this stage of change. Don't stop here. A person in this stage doesn't know how to apply the information effectively and she may stay stuck for many years accumu-

lating books describing what she wishes for in a relationship. A pers...
veloping awareness lacks the ability to turn the information into a practi...
plan of action. When she does take action, because it is without a plan, she
will often give up at the first sign of difficulty or disappointment, and return
to the safety of what is not satisfactory, but is familiar.

STRATEGIES

A person developing awareness needs more consciousness-raising. Consciousness-raising allows her to learn about the costs of remaining with the status quo. Further, it helps her to project the outcome of continuing to behave in a way that supports the present situation remaining as it is. A person developing awareness needs to surround herself with other people who are on a similar journey. This helps her to develop healthy, realistic goals. Further, hearing about others' journeys as they grow usually helps with increasing options for her own growth. **A healthy support system removes a mental and emotional degree of difficulty that frequently comes with isolation, specifically feelings of shame and pathology (there is something wrong with me, my partner, or us), which make the process of growth harder than it needs to be.**

3. PLANNING APPLICATION OF AWARENESS, PLANNING ACTION

A person at this stage is planning to take action. He has hope, and oftentimes a general plan, and is building momentum.

STRATEGIES

A person in this stage needs a firm plan of action. This plan of action should be:

- In writing
- Stated in the positive
- Have specific action strategies that are observable and measurable
- Have remedies for setbacks and for revision
- Have specific dates for evaluation

This person should brainstorm his goals with a supportive group of helpful people. He shouldn't include anyone who is not helpful or anyone who is overly negative.

If immediate family and friends are not helpful, use the strength and resourcefulness of a self-help group. Every community has free or inexpensive self-help groups through mental health agencies, nonprofit agencies, churches, and peer community movements. Positive social support and feedback play critical roles in this stage.

4. TAKING THOUGHTFUL ACTION

A person in this stage is moving her body through space in a way consistent with her action plan. Action means observable and measurable behavioral change. Sometimes action is clumsy or awkward, but it's usually a step in the right direction because it stretches an individual and provides feedback. Action "disturbs" the system in some way that will invite change, growth, or increased awareness. This information is important for further growth.

STRATEGIES

This person needs to mindfully do more, do less, or try some different behavior altogether. Thoughtful action adds information and opens up options. **She should notice and appreciate small accomplishments with her partner and her support network.**

She should remember that any new pattern feels unfamiliar at first. These are new habits and new neural information that her brain is processing. Do it one day at a time. Recommit every day to the process of growth. Remember that she is changing months, and probably years, of worn out negative behaviors and thoughts. She should commit to repetition of the desired patterns, until they become hers. (In ballroom dance, they say it takes 600 to 900 repetitions for a dance step to become yours.)

5. USING THOUGHTFUL FEEDBACK

In order to grow a person needs data from his actions. He needs to ask himself questions, such as:

- What is different in my behaviors, thoughts, and feelings since I started my planned changes?
- What is different in my partner, my environment, and the people around me?
- Is it predictably difficult?
- Is anything better? Is anything worse?
- Have I taken too large a step too fast? Do I need to slow down?
- Do I need to give it more time?

Making course adjustments along the way is normal. A plan without the benefit of feedback is not a complete plan and it is too rigid.

STRATEGIES

This person should set aside a regular, specific reflection and feedback time either alone, with his partner, or his support network. It may be daily, weekly, or monthly depending on what he is addressing.

- Notice what is working differently
- Notice what is working well
- Notice the absence of problems
- Notice what he is doing, how it feels, what his thought process is
- Notice what he wants to do more of, what he wants to interrupt or change, and how

Put feedback summaries in writing. This stage is for making well thought-out adjustments to the action plan.

6. MAINTENANCE PLAN

Maintaining a healthy relationship is the repetition of thoughtful patterns of growing awareness, planning action, taking action, and using feedback. Maintenance will last a lifetime.

Individuals who desire easy change (I believe that is an oxymoron), or a one-time change ignore the fact that maintaining a healthy relationship is a continuous process. Common challenges to maintenance are:

- We stop doing what works because the situation has improved
- The harmful listlessness of the default setting of old patterns returns
- We sustain situational imbalances (such as job loss, new baby, new job, illness, move, or loss) that challenge health and wellness routines or behaviors
- We become out of balance in some significant way without remembering to employ a mindful reset button.

STRATEGIES

A person in maintenance should apply similar strategies to those used in the action and feedback phases:

- Mindfulness
- Taking time for feedback and reflection
- Brainstorming options to unproductive behaviors
- Putting goals in positive terms in writing
- Continuing to nurture supportive relationships

Keep in mind this "Which Stage of Growth Are You In?" template as you consider the different areas of your relationship. It can help with building an effective plan for couple enrichment.

WHICH STAGE OF RELATIONSHIP GROWTH ARE YOU IN?
(Sample worksheet)

Use this form to evaluate where you each are in the growth process as it relates to a specific dimension of your couples relationship.

DIMENSION OR AREA OF FOCUS:

Example: Nonverbal communication

Check the readiness of each partner. Write what your priorities, goals, and challenges are for each of you to process effectively the stages you are in relative to a specific dimension.

READINESS:

PARTNER A: MATT   **PARTNER B: SUSAN**

√   Undeveloped Awareness

Developing Awareness   √

Planning Application of Awareness

Action Plan

Feedback

Revised Action Plan

Feedback

Revised Action Plan

Feedback

This repetition is called Maintenance

If you are in different stages, are you aware of it? And, are you working respectfully with each other on that issue? If you are not, then that may be one source of distance or conflict in the relationship. If you are in different stages, how do you respect each other's developmental needs?

1. *Matt will read three short articles on body language, facial expressions, and tone within ten days of this date (check for resources on the internet).*

2. *Matt and Susan agree to a verbal cue, "let's take a snapshot" to stop and notice body language from each member and name how it feels (Where do you feel it in your body?). What would you name the emotion(s)? If it is not appropriate to do it in the moment, then do it sometime in the next twenty-four hours after a data point "snapshot."*

3. *We will each come up with a list of three nonverbal skills to work on and will share that information with the other. Each partner will rate his or her level (on a scale from 0 to 10, where 0 = no skills at all and 10 = fabulous skills) at the beginning of this process. Rescale weekly to show the level each partner feels he or she has grown to.*

Matt: 1) Stop and focus fully on partner, 2) Take a breath, 3) Make eye contact. Initial scaling point: 3.

Susan: 1) Stop and focus fully on partner, 2) Take a breath, 3) Notice him focusing on me and taking a breath and making eye contact, and 4) Put my hand on my heart to bring awareness to my tone of voice. Initial scaling point: 6.

How does each of you struggle with this issue of different developmental stages on the same dimension?

Matt: I feel less than. I feel reprimanded. I feel wrong.

Susan: I feel angry. I feel not good enough. I feel like I am being petty.

What can you do together about this?

Matt: I will check and ask Susan if she feels what we are doing together is important. I will ask if she thinks less of me each time I start to notice these feelings and thoughts getting in my way. Better yet, I will ask before any of these feelings get in our way.

Susan: I will check and ask Matt if he feels what we are doing together is important. I will express appreciation for our work together.

What can you do individually about this?

Matt: I will read for two minutes daily on nonverbal communication elements to keep my awareness growing.

Susan: I will count my blessings daily. I will take two minutes to list three things we have each done well or tried in the last two days to improve nonverbal communication awareness and skill use.

What specific supportive words, actions, or thoughts can you each use to increase the likelihood of a more positive outcome (or even a less negative outcome) on this dimension? Be specific. Describe the actual words that will be more helpful.

1. Matt or Susan: Let's take a snapshot of this moment to learn from later.

2. Matt or Susan: I would like a moment to finish what I am doing so I can give you my full attention.

3. Matt or Susan: Let me know when you are available for a brief conversation about xyz in the next 30 minutes.

Describe the specific actions that will be more helpful. (Where? When? By whom?)

Matt: Come into the same room or area and sit facing each other. I prefer the kitchen (if no one else is around) or bedroom.

Susan: Put my hand on my heart before I speak. Touch my partner's hand if possible.

Matt and Susan: We will discuss this for ten minutes weekly, Saturday mornings sometime between 10:00 and 11:00.

Describe the specific thoughts you would like to have to replace negative draining thoughts that perpetuate old patterns.

Matt and Susan:

1. "This is hopeless" is replaced by "We can do this together."

2. "This is silly or pointless" is replaced by "The immediate benefits of this are: 1) Working together, 2) Feeling more connected to each other, 3) Fewer misunderstandings."

3. "We should not need to do this" is replaced by "I have a partner I can grow with."

WHICH STAGE OF RELATIONSHIP GROWTH ARE YOU IN?

Use this form to evaluate where you each are in the growth process as it relates to a specific dimension of your couples relationship.

DIMENSION OR AREA OF FOCUS:

Check the readiness of each partner. Write what your priorities, goals, and challenges are for each of you to process effectively the stages you are in relative to a specific dimension.

READINESS:

PARTNER A   **PARTNER B**

Undeveloped Awareness

Developing Awareness

Planning Application of Awareness

Action Plan

Feedback

Revised Action Plan

Feedback

Revised Action Plan

Feedback

This repetition is called Maintenance

If you are in different stages, are you aware of it? And, are you working respectfully with each other on that issue? If you are not, then that may be one source of distance or conflict in the relationship. If you are in different stages, how do you respect each other's developmental needs?

How does each of you struggle with this issue of different developmental stages on the same dimension?

What can you do together about this?

What can you do individually about this?

What specific supportive words, actions, or thoughts can you each use to increase the likelihood of a more positive outcome (or even a less negative outcome) on this dimension? Be specific. Describe the actual words that will be more helpful.

Describe the specific actions that will be more helpful. (Where? When? By whom?)

Describe the specific thoughts you would like to have to replace negative draining thoughts that perpetuate old patterns.

CHAPTER 6

BASIC COMMUNICATION
Part 1

This is a daily, hourly, and by the minute needed skill set.

The communication chapters are my lens. My lens comes from exposure to the research and work of some of the leaders in the field of marriage and the family:

- **John Gottman: http://www.gottman.com**
- **Howard Markman: http://www.loveyourrelationship.com**
- **David Olsen: http://www.prepare-enrich.com**
- **David Schnarch: http://www.passionatemarriage.com**
- **Richard Schwartz: http://www.selfleadership.org**
- **Michele Weiner-Davis: http://www.divorcebusting.com**
- **Michael White: http://www.dulwichcentre.com.au**

GOAL AND STYLES

What would be the most important chapter of a couples book? How to get more sex? How to get better sex? How to be more loving with each other? How to get more romance? *Yes* and *no*. It is about sex, love, and romance. It all starts and ends with communication.

GOAL OF COMMUNICATION:

*The goal of communication is
to share information
and more importantly
to build connection.*

It is vital to attend to how you communicate and to assess the quality of that communication. Communication is an effective lubricant for relationships; it helps them run smoother and feel better. Effective communication is ergonomic; it improves a couple's fit.

When communication is working well there are fewer misunderstandings. When there are differences they are shared more effectively and processed more easily. Similarities are shared at a deeper level.

When you and your partner communicate well, it doesn't mean you agree with each other. Sometimes you agree to disagree. Effective communication certainly doesn't mean giving up a sense of oneself. In fact, just the opposite is true.

A good communicator shares oneself as well as attends
to learning about the other person.

Communication is not about winning or losing.

Positive communication is respectful, inclusive, and
empowering for each member.

Critical Reminder: Just as you change clothes when you get home, you need to change roles. Examples of this are the military, law enforcement, attorneys, physicians, teachers, nurses, executive assistants, therapists, managers, and so on. The distinct communication skill set you use effectively in your role at work, particularly if it is a specialized career, will not necessarily transfer to a personal setting. In all likelihood, you will have to leave your work demeanor at work. Some general skills will transfer; however, being in manager mode, attorney mode, detective mode, or military mode when you get home will hurt, not help, your coupleship and your family.

BASIC COMMUNICATION OVERVIEW

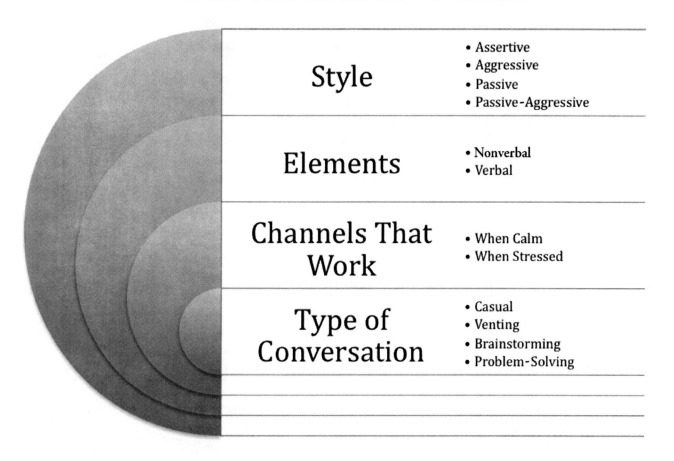

Style	• Assertive • Aggressive • Passive • Passive-Aggressive
Elements	• Nonverbal • Verbal
Channels That Work	• When Calm • When Stressed
Type of Conversation	• Casual • Venting • Brainstorming • Problem-Solving

STYLES OF COMMUNICATION:

There are four styles of communication:

- Assertive
- Aggressive
- Passive
- Passive-Aggressive

Only the assertive style of communication works well for couples, families, intimacy, and health.

Assertiveness is a learned skill. Communication skills are influenced by early childhood environment, and communication skills continue to evolve and develop through the school years and beyond. Many adults learn additional communication skills as part of career development. If you did not grow up with effective communication skills, it will take effort to acquire them. It is worth the effort.

Here is a brief description of each communication style.

Assertive people are direct, clear, and to the point. Assertive people use "I" statements rather than "You" statements. They are not afraid to respectfully share their views, opinions, and preferences. They are open to experiencing other people sharing their views. They listen as much as they speak. It is stimulating and fun to interact with assertive people.

Aggressive people are direct, sometimes clear, and infrequently to the point. Aggressive people use "You" messages. They are quick to label, blame, and take umbrage. They rely on intimidation and power to make their point. They are not interested in other's views or opinions. They are "right." They are not good listeners. When they do listen, it is for the purpose of rebuttal, argument, and winning. It is draining to interact with or even to just witness aggressive people in action.

Passive people are neither direct, clear, nor to the point. Passive people refrain from sharing their views and preferences. Passive people hide who they are by going along and superficially getting along with whatever the other wants. It is uninteresting and tiring to be around passive people.

Passive-Aggressive people are knowingly and unknowingly dishonest, usually because in their formative years they did not feel safe to express their preferences and opinions. Appearing passive and pursuing what they secretly want is a style that probably protected them in the past. Without personal insight and growth, the continued pattern will hurt them and those around them in any significant relationships. It is frustrating and maddening to be around passive-aggressive people.

What do you think would be some of the relationship difficulties if you paired together the different styles of communicators?

For more information on assertiveness, I recommend *Your Perfect Right: Assertiveness and Equity in Your Life and Relationships* (9th edition), 2008, by Robert E. Alberti and Michael L. Emmons.

A Brief Advertisement for Assertiveness Skills:

COST OF NONASSERTIVE COMMUNICATION STYLES

MORE
- **Misunderstandings**
- **Anger and Resentment**
- **Parenting Problems**
- **Health Problems**
- **Breakups and Divorces**

Lost Time Spent Battling without Resolution

Money and Time – Greater Resources Spent on Relationship Managing Experts Such as Coaches, Individual Therapists, Marriage Therapists, Mediators, Attorneys

Cost of assertiveness training and proper use:

PRICELESS

EVALUATING YOURSELF AS A COMMUNICATOR IN YOUR COUPLES RELATIONSHIP (Partner A)

The Four Styles: Assertive, Aggressive, Passive, Passive-Aggressive

Notice your communication style under different circumstances.

What is your primary communication style at work on an average day (whether you work inside or outside the home)?

What is your primary communication style at work on a difficult day?

What is your primary communication style publicly with your partner?

What is your primary communication style privately with your partner?

What is your primary communication style in the bedroom?

Does your communication style change when you are under stress? To what other style?

If it does change, and not for the better, you can notice when that change occurs and use it as a road sign that you can interpret as: Stressed: No need to make it worse.

What would your partner say your primary communication style is with her?

If your partner describes your communication style differently than you do, how do you account for the difference?

If your partner answers the question at a time of smooth communication, chances are there is merit in her perceptions.

What communication styles were modeled by significant people in your early years?

Who modeled which styles?

How did you feel when you were at the receiving end of each communication style?

	Better	Worse
Assertive		
Aggressive		
Passive		
Passive-Aggressive		

Do you want to learn to be more assertive with your partner?

What would be the benefits of being more assertive with your partner?

For her? For you?

Do you want your partner to be more assertive with you?

What would be the benefits of having a more assertive partner?

What would be the challenges? How will you discuss the challenges when they occur?

Let her know what your intention is. <u>Do it in writing</u>.

EVALUATING YOURSELF AS A COMMUNICATOR IN YOUR COUPLES RELATIONSHIP (Partner B)

The Four Styles: Assertive, Aggressive, Passive, Passive-Aggressive

Notice your communication style under different circumstances.

What is your primary communication style at work on an average day (whether you work inside or outside the home)?

What is your primary communication style at work on a difficult day?

What is your primary communication style publicly with your partner?

What is your primary communication style privately with your partner?

What is your primary communication style in the bedroom?

Does your communication style change when you are under stress? To what other style?

If it does change, and not for the better, you can notice when that change occurs and use it as a road sign that you can interpret as: Stressed: No need to make it worse.

What would your partner say your primary communication style is with her?

If your partner describes your communication style differently than you do, how do you account for the difference?

If your partner answers the question at a time of smooth communication, chances are there is merit in her perceptions.

What communication styles were modeled by significant people in your early years?

Who modeled which styles?

How did you feel when you were at the receiving end of each communication style?

	Better	Worse
Assertive		
Aggressive		
Passive		
Passive-Aggressive		

Do you want to learn to be more assertive with your partner?

What would be the benefits of being more assertive with your partner?

For her? For you?

Do you want your partner to be more assertive with you?

What would be the benefits of having a more assertive partner?

What would be the challenges? How will you discuss the challenges when they occur?

Let her know what your intention is. <u>Do it in writing</u>.

CHAPTER 7

BASIC COMMUNICATION
Part 2

This is a daily, hourly, and by the minute needed skill set.

Communication Elements: Verbal and Nonverbal

There is no such thing as not being able to communicate. Even not communicating is a form of communication. It often means something negative such as "I am angry," "I am hurt," "I am overwhelmed," or "no."

Examples of *not* communicating are:

- Not responding
- Not answering
- Changing the subject
- Saying you will address it later, but there is never an actual time; you continue to avoid
- Ignoring your partner
- Continuing to put your partner off when she brings up a subject you want to ignore

Communication is verbal and nonverbal. Nonverbal communication includes:

- Setting the stage
- Listening attentively
- Eye contact
- Facial expressions
- Body language

Verbal communication consists of:

- Using words and tones that invite listening
- Being clear and to the point, being brief

A majority of couples misunderstandings are about not hearing and understanding what your partner has shared with you because too often both of you are multitasking, distracted, wanting to be heard at the same time, or just not paying attention.

NONVERBAL COMMUNICATION SKILL 1

Setting the Stage for an Important Discussion:
Brainstorming, Problem Solving, or Venting

1. Use a setting that invites calm and has minimal distractions. Turn off the television, radio, computers, phones, cell phones, smart phones, electronic games, etc., so you are free from interruptions. Create the same tone as a therapy session or an important business meeting. This time together is important. Your relationship is important. Treat it that way.

2. Have an agreed upon time and location to meet that is beneficial for both of you. Take one or two minutes to settle yourself before the meeting.

3. Sit comfortably together, one should not be looming over the other. Eye contact and touch should be possible.

4. Keep the meeting to forty-five minutes or less. If you need more time, schedule a follow up meeting.

5. Have an agreed upon agenda.

6. Limit yourselves to one topic per meeting, which usually keeps most meetings well under the time limit.

7. Don't partake of alcohol or other substances. Don't have important discussions over a glass of wine.

8. Don't have a meeting when one or both of you are hungry, angry, late, tired, or sick (HALTS). It's better to reschedule for when you're both rested enough to give the dialogue and each other your full attention.

9. If you are tense, do something relaxing such as taking a walk, taking a shower, or exercising before meeting time. Sometimes you can do this together, sometimes not.

NONVERBAL SKILL 2

Listening Attentively: Listening with the Intention of Connection

Listening with acknowledgment means giving your *full attention* to and working on hearing what your partner has to say *to her satisfaction.* Check in on what you are hearing (for accuracy of hearing, not argument, agreement, or rebuttal) when your partner pauses, every two to five sentences.

Checking in sounds like "What I heard you say is. . .; Is that accurate?" If she says "No," ask her to make her point again, perhaps with fewer sentences so you can understand her to her satisfaction.

1. Check in with yourself before you start listening. Are you ready to give your partner your full attention?

2. Take a minute to slow down so you can be present and available for yourself, your partner, and the topic. Close your eyes and take a couple of slow deep breaths. Notice your breath or your heartbeat.

3. Bring your attention to your partner's face and what she wants to share.

4. When she pauses, every three or four sentences, check in with her on what you understand she's saying. This is simply an acknowledgment of her feelings and thoughts.

Acknowledgment does not mean agreement. You don't give up any power or your point of view by acknowledging your partner's position. More likely, you gain respect from your partner because you're giving respect to your partner.

Listening attentively is not about argument, rebuttal, excuses, rationalizations, explanations, answers, getting the record straight, correcting, or any other righteous reasons.

Listening attentively is not about you. It is about your partner and her thoughts, feelings, concerns, worries.

Listening attentively is a skill we all need.

Chances are it's a skill you already have. There are people and situations where you use the skill automatically without having to work at it. With colleagues at work, clients, a close friend, or someone you respect such as a mentor or role model. In all likelihood, you are able to listen to your partner if you believe the information she wants to share is positive or valuable.

If you do not have adequate listening skills, read about listening skills at http://www.wikihow.com/Be-a-Good-Listener. Begin practicing genuine listening as often as you can, wherever you can. You need it in most significant relationships in your life with parents, kids, siblings, colleagues, friends, and acquaintances.

What reminders do you need to practice effective listening skills with your partner?

- Make a cue card ahead of time to keep you focused on listening.
- Use a talking object if one of you has a habit of interrupting, or talking over the other. A talking object is a fob or stuffed animal you pass back and forth, whoever has it is the one speaking, and the other person gets to listen.
- Hold a roll of duct tape to remind yourself to use your ears and your heart rather than your mouth and your ego. Let your partner know why you brought the duct tape to the conversation—specifically, to be a better listener.

Do what it takes to listen to your significant other to her satisfaction.

NONVERBAL SKILL 3
Eye Contact

Sit in such a way that you can make attentive eye contact with your partner as he speaks. The obvious reminders are no eye rolling (do you even know if you do it?), no glaring, or staring. Listening to someone while staring over his shoulder, at his chest, or at your own hands, conveys unavailability. An avoidance of eye contact is an avoidance of connection.

Some cultures permit eye contact only in specific relationships. If eye contact is a cross-cultural issue then it needs to be a topic of discussion to brainstorm and resolve as a couple. If it's not a cross-cultural issue, learn and practice attentive eye contact with your partner.

NONVERBAL SKILL 4

Facial Expressions

Facial expressions, similar to voice tone, can be difficult to notice and elusive to resolve. If your partner says that your facial expressions feel hostile, and he's sincere, believe him. Whether or not anger or hostility is the message you are intending to convey, it's the message he is receiving. Helpful adjustments may be to meet in a public place, use a mirror for yourself for facial feedback, or include a *caring neutral and skilled party* (not a close friend or family member), such as a therapist, coach, mentor, monk, rabbi, priest, or minister (one that has wisdom about relationships), to be a witness to the conversation.

NONVERBAL SKILL 5

Body Language

Body language that conveys hostility or inattentiveness is not effective in communicating teamwork, collaboration, or respect. Don't loom over your partner. Try to be roughly eye-to-eye. Turning away from your partner while he is speaking, tensely crossed limbs, unexplained fidgeting, or restlessness convey disinterest.

Again, physical exercise, a shower, meditation, a mirror, a public setting, or a third party witness may be helpful in the short term to facilitate a change of pattern.

VERBAL SKILL 1

Speaking with the Intention of Connecting

Check in with yourself before you start speaking. Take a minute to slow down so you can be present and available for yourself, your partner, and the topic. Close your eyes and take a couple of deep slow breaths. Notice your breath or your heartbeat. Then bring your attention to the *one specific issue* you would like to address.

If you can't slow down enough to do this, if you are piling on multiple issues, then you're not ready to communicate effectively with your partner.

A general rule of thumb is on a scale of 0 to 10, with 0 = no charge or totally calm and 10 = uncontrolled pure melt down. Try to address issues when they're at a charge of 6.5 or less and preferably at 5 or below. This means address issues as they emerge in a relationship; remember that timing is important. Don't wait for issues to build in intensity. Too much emotional intensity prevents effective communication.

What should you do if you are at a six on this scale and moving up or at a solid seven or more? Take a break, using exercise or some form of activity to reduce the charge. **The negative emotions have a brain and body chemistry (the flight or fight response of the parasympathetic nervous system) that will undermine and complicate any efforts to communicate by triggering the natural self-defense system of the listener.**

So if you want your partner to hear you, be in a nonaggressive, nonthreatened, and nonthreatening place.

If an issue triggers you to a point where you cannot communicate effectively, try first talking to a caring neutral party.

When your emotional intensity is at five or below, that is the time to address an issue. If you can't get to a five with any regularity, then it's time to work with a marriage counselor.

When you are ready (at five or below), bring awareness to your tone of voice and your choice of words.

VERBAL SKILL 2

Be Brief: Speak Clearly and to the Point

Use two to five sentences at a time. Then stop and check with your partner for listening quality and acknowledgment. If he doesn't understand what you just said, don't go on. Instead, repeat your point until he has heard you to your satisfaction.

If this doesn't work after three tries, you can write your sentences for you and your partner to read aloud. If your partner still can't follow you then it's time to consult a marriage counselor. Not hearing you may be about anger, resentment, and a power struggle between the two of you. It's probably a bigger issue than the issue you are trying to discuss.

Many couples cite "communication problems" as the issue when they first come to marriage therapy. "Communication problems" have a whole array of structural issues such as the skills I am discussing in Chapters 5 through 9. In addition, "communication problems" have an array of fuel to feed the fires of disharmony, which are the subjects of Chapters 11 through 17.

SUMMARY OF VERBAL AND NONVERBAL COMMUNICATION TOOLS

Nonverbal Skill 1: Setting the Stage

- Agreed upon time (forty-five minute limit)
- Agreed upon location
- Agreed upon topic (one per meeting), be prepared to participate as a speaker and a listener
- No interruptions, electronics and communication devices off or silenced
- No alcohol or substance
- No HALTS (hungry, angry, late, tired, sick)
- In preparation exercise, meditate or shower before

Nonverbal Skill 2: Listening Attentively

- Give your partner your full intention, eyes, ears, heart, breath, brain
- Check in for understanding only

Nonverbal Skill 3: Appropriate eye contact

Nonverbal Skill 4: Appropriate facial expressions

Nonverbal Skill 5: Appropriate body language

- Calm, Safe, Open
- Same eye level
- Attentive

Verbal Skills:

- Appropriate volume
- Appropriate tone
- Appropriate language
- Speak clearly and to the point
- Take a break every three or four sentences to check for understanding

NONVERBAL SKILL 1 (Partner A)

SETTING THE STAGE

How are you at setting the stage? What are two or three skills you already use? Be specific.

1.

2.

3.

Are there times, places or circumstances where these skills work better than others with your partner? What is the difference? Be specific.

Do you use these skills effectively with other people? Be specific. Who? Where?

What are one or two of your "setting the stage" challenges? Be specific.
What can you do differently during those challenging situations in order to have communication that is more effective with your partner? Be specific.

	CHALLENGE	REMEDY
1.		
2.		

What do you need to do in order to remember to use these new or adjusted "setting the stage" skills?

1.

2.

3.

Remember you have choice
in each moment

NONVERBAL SKILL 1 (Partner B)

SETTING THE STAGE

How are you at setting the stage? What are two or three skills you already use? Be specific.

1.

2.

3.

Are there times, places or circumstances where these skills work better than others with your partner? What is the difference? Be specific.

Do you use these skills effectively with other people? Be specific. Who? Where?

What are one or two of your "setting the stage" challenges? Be specific.
What can you do differently during those challenging situations in order to have communication that is more effective with your partner? Be specific.

	CHALLENGE	REMEDY
1.		
2.		

What do you need to do in order to remember to use these new or adjusted "setting the stage" skills?

1.

2.

3.

Remember you have choice
in each moment

NONVERBAL SKILLS 2 - 5 (Partner A)

LISTENING ATTENTIVELY, LISTENING WITH THE INTENT OF CONNECTION, EYE CONTACT, FACIAL EXPRESSIONS, AND BODY LANGUAGE

On a scale of 1 to 5:

> 1 = very poor
> 2 = somewhat poor
> 3 = mostly adequate
> 4 = very adequate
> 5 = excellent, this is not a problem

Mark in one color where you presently are in each of these areas. Then in a different color mark where you want to be in the next week or month. Make it a realistic and do-able goal. Make a brief note on how you will achieve your goal. (Use additional paper if necessary.)

If it is possible, do you stop what you are doing to listen to your partner?

| 1 | 2 | 3 | 4 | 5 |

Do you give your partner your fullest possible attention?

| 1 | 2 | 3 | 4 | 5 |

Are you in the same room with your partner? Are you facing your partner? Do you make eye contact? Is it a quick glance or do you look into your partner's eyes?

| 1 | 2 | 3 | 4 | 5 |

Are you aware of your facial expressions? Has your partner mentioned your facial expressions as an issue?

| 1 | 2 | 3 | 4 | 5 |

Does your body language convey listening, receiving, and openness?

| 1 | 2 | 3 | 4 | 5 |

If it is not a good time to be attentive, do you share that information and set an appropriate time that has some immediacy, such as in ten minutes? In thirty minutes? Tomorrow at 2:00 p.m.?

| 1 | 2 | 3 | 4 | 5 |

When you set a more appropriate time, do you keep your word? If you say "In a minute," do you actually take a minute? Figures of speech are neither helpful nor accurate. Use your time words carefully and accurately.

| 1 | 2 | 3 | 4 | 5 |

Listen to your partner with still attention,
with spaciousness

NONVERBAL SKILLS 2 - 5 (Partner B)

LISTENING ATTENTIVELY, LISTENING WITH THE INTENT OF CONNECTION, EYE CONTACT, FACIAL EXPRESSIONS, AND BODY LANGUAGE

On a scale of 1 to 5:

> 1 = very poor
> 2 = somewhat poor
> 3 = mostly adequate
> 4 = very adequate
> 5 = excellent, this is not a problem

Mark in one color where you presently are in each of these areas. Then in a different color, mark where you want to be in the next week or month. Make it a realistic and doable goal. Make a brief note on how you will achieve your goal. (Use additional paper if necessary.)

If it is possible, do you stop what you are doing to listen to your partner?

1   2   3   4   5

Do you give your partner your fullest possible attention?

1   2   3   4   5

Are you in the same room with your partner? Are you facing your partner? Do you make eye contact? Is it a quick glance or do you look into your partner's eyes?

1   2   3   4   5

Are you aware of your facial expressions? Has your partner mentioned your facial expressions as an issue?

1   2   3   4   5

Does your body language convey listening, receiving and openness?

1   2   3   4   5

If it is not a good time to be attentive, do you share that information and set an appropriate time that has some immediacy, such as in ten minutes? In thirty minutes? Tomorrow at 2:00 p.m.?

1   2   3   4   5

When you set a more appropriate time, do you keep your word? If you say "In a minute," do you actually take a minute? Figures of speech are neither helpful nor accurate. Use your time words carefully and accurately.

1   2   3   4   5

43

Listen to your partner with still attention,
with spaciousness

VERBAL SKILLS (Partner A)

On a scale of 1 to 5:

    1 = very poor
    2 = somewhat poor
    3 = mostly adequate
    4 = very adequate
    5 = excellent, this is not a problem

Mark in one color where you presently are in each of these areas. Then in a different color mark where you want to be in the next week or month. Make it a realistic and doable goal. Make a brief note on how you will achieve your goal. (Use additional paper if necessary.)

When you initiate a discussion, do you limit the discussion to one issue?

    1   **2**   **3**   **4**   **5**

Are you aware of your tone? Has your partner mentioned your tone as an issue?

    1   **2**   **3**   **4**   **5**

What are three things <u>you can do</u> to improve your awareness of your tone and to improve your tone?

    1.

    2.

    3.

Are you aware of your volume? Has your partner mentioned your volume as an issue?

    1   **2**   **3**   **4**   **5**

What are three things <u>you can do</u> to be a more effective communicator with your volume?

    1.

    2.

    3.

Are you aware of your language? Do you name-call? Do you curse? Do you use sarcasm?

1   **2**   **3**   **4**   **5**

What are five things you can do instead of name-calling, cursing, or sarcasm?

1.

2.

3.

4.

5.

Make an amends chart that you both can benefit from. This is not about punishment or shaming. It is about putting your intention into action by including motivational consequences and remedies.

Keep toothpicks, dried beans, or matches around for difficult discussions. Have you and your partner keep track of how many times you name-call and curse by moving one bean into a cup for each infraction. Make amends to your partner for each infraction by doing extra household chores, especially chores your partner would love to pass on. At a time of easy communication, make an amends chart similar to the following.

One bean = make the bed in the morning

Two beans = do the dishes after dinner

Three beans = clean the bathroom

Four beans = . . .

You get the point.

After you answer these questions for yourself, ask your partner to answer them based on his experiences with you.

From the combined information, develop a communication improvement plan in writing for yourself. Give a copy to your partner. Review it together weekly for a month. If communication is better, then review it monthly for a quarter. If more effective communication becomes a habit, and you are using the skills regularly, then there is little need for review of those skills since you now practice them daily. You can set a different goal or use the time for fun.

Any time communication gets difficult pull the review sheet out. If communication does get difficult or less effective, if pernicious old habits are returning, it does not mean the tools are not working. More likely, the tools are not being employed or there are complicating factors that need additional tools.

VERBAL SKILLS (Partner B)

On a scale of 1 to 5:

    1 = very poor
    2 = somewhat poor
    3 = mostly adequate
    4 = very adequate
    5 = excellent, this is not a problem

Mark in one color where you presently are in each of these areas. Then in a different color mark where you want to be in the next week or month. Make it a realistic and doable goal. Make a brief note on how you will achieve your goal. (Use additional paper if necessary.)

When you initiate a discussion, do you limit the discussion to one issue?

    1   **2**   **3**   **4**   **5**

Are you aware of your tone? Has your partner mentioned your tone as an issue?

    1   **2**   **3**   **4**   **5**

What are three things <u>you can do</u> to improve your awareness of your tone and to improve your tone?

    1.

    2.

    3.

Are you aware of your volume? Has your partner mentioned your volume as an issue?

    1   **2**   **3**   **4**   **5**

What are three things <u>you can do</u> to be a more effective communicator with your volume?

    1.

    2.

    3.

Are you aware of your language? Do you name-call? Do you curse? Do you use sarcasm?

1   **2**   **3**   **4**   **5**

What are five things you can do instead of name-calling, cursing, or sarcasm?

1.

2.

3.

4.

5.

Make an amends chart that you both can benefit from. This is not about punishment or shaming. It is about putting your intention into action by including motivational consequences and remedies.

Keep toothpicks, dried beans, or matches around for difficult discussions. Have you and your partner keep track of how many times you name-call and curse by moving one bean into a cup for each infraction. Make amends to your partner for each infraction by doing extra household chores, especially chores your partner would love to pass on. At a time of easy communication, make an amends chart similar to the following.

One bean = make the bed in the morning

Two beans = do the dishes after dinner

Three beans = clean the bathroom

Four beans = . . .

You get the point.

After you answer these questions for yourself, ask your partner to answer them based on his experiences with you.

From the combined information, develop a communication improvement plan in writing for yourself. Give a copy to your partner. Review it together weekly for a month. If communication is better, then review it monthly for a quarter. If more effective communication becomes a habit, and you are using the skills regularly, then there is little need for review of those skills since you now practice them daily. You can set a different goal or use the time for fun.

Any time communication gets difficult pull the review sheet out. If communication does get difficult or less effective, if pernicious old habits are returning, it does not mean the tools are not working. More likely, the tools are not being employed or there are complicating factors that need additional tools.

CHAPTER 8

PERSONAL COMMUNICATION STYLES

This is a daily needed skill set.

CHANNELS THAT WORK AND CHANNELS THAT DO NOT WORK

Frequently, the message sender attempts to communicate with the partner in a manner that suits the message sender rather than the message receiver. If you take just a moment to think about this idea, you can see how anti-ergonomic and crazy this proposition is.

Matt likes physical touch when he communicates with his partner, Susan. Holding her hand helps Matt feel connected. Susan, however, does not like touch before she is ready. For her, having Matt hold her hand before she is ready, feels intrusive and controlling. So, if Matt wants to have effective communication with Susan, what does he need to do? And, if Susan wants to have effective communication with Matt, what does she need to do?

Answers: When Matt is attempting to communicate something important to Susan, he needs to use her style. No touch until invited. When Susan is attempting to communicate something important to Matt, she needs to use his style. Hold his hand while talking to him.

The unscientific analogy I use is that one partner is on an AM radio frequency and the other is on FM. **When your partner is on a different frequency, turning up the volume on your own frequency is ineffective, inefficient, and stressful for both parties.**

Learn about your partner's communication frequency.

At a time of easy flowing communication and low stress, ask about your partner's communication preferences; areas with varying preferences such as:

- Time of day
- Preparation time needed before
- Percolating time needed during or after
- Sitting in one place versus going for a walk
- The use of touch with communication

After learning about his preferences, share your own. Put each person's preferences in writing as part of your relationship guide.

Here are some examples.

Time of Day

- I am a morning person. After 7:00 a.m. and before 10:00 a.m. is best.
- Afternoons are not good. I am at my lowest then.
- Evenings, after dinner and up to 8:00 p.m. are good most of the time.
- I prefer to talk before the kids get up.
- I would like to address difficult issues on Saturday mornings.

Preparation Time before Discussion

- I prefer forty-eight hours notice if it is a difficult topic for me or us.
- I would like to talk after my parents leave.
- I would like to plan a check-in conversation time while we walk in the morning for the whole week we are on vacation.
- I would like to have regular discussion times planned for twice a week so issues don't build up. How about having a regular check-in couples time Thursday mornings between 6:15 and 6:45?

Percolating Time

When you have two individuals, it's unlikely that they process information at the same rate. Respecting the different percolating times is important in including both voices in any discussion.

There is no right or wrong amount of time. Partners should respect each other's different processing timeframes and develop acceptance and tolerance of each of their individual percolating rates.

This is similar to left-handedness and right-handedness. There is not a correct way, and it's unlikely that you can coerce your partner into adapting your style. Don't pick percolating times as an issue to fight about or have a power struggle over. The quicker percolator needs to self-soothe (meaning to relieve or ease pain or discomfort) and take a breath while her partner is percolating.

What timeframe works for you? What timeframe works for your partner? How do you respect both processing speeds?

"When you come to me with an issue, problem, or just want my opinion, because you are important to me, and I want to give it quality thought, I need some time to think about the topic before I respond to you. I'd like (how many minutes or hours) to percolate before I get back to you." This timeframe may vary by topic and context.

It is common for a person to need a few hours to percolate; even to sleep on it. The percolating person negotiates a specific time (within twenty-four hours in most cases) to return to the topic.

Yes, the slower person gets more influence about timing in this situation because the slower percolator needs more time to be effective in sharing his perspective. Percolating time is not an avoidance technique. The purpose of percolating time is to be more thoughtful and present.

If either of you believe it's an avoidance technique or being used as an avoidance technique, then that should be brought up as a couple's discussion topic. Understand how you as a couple want percolating time to work for your mutual benefit.

Touch

The use of appropriate touch in effective communication is a critical modality to understand and negotiate. How does each of you want to be touched in different circumstances? How? When? Where? Demonstrate what works for you in different circumstances. Have your partner practice what you demonstrate and what works for you. Do the same for your partner. Remember, touch may be affected by hormones and fatigue; one answer may not fit for all times.

It is common for either partner to have very specific preferences in some areas of communication and have easy broad flexibility in others. We have the fact of our unique preferences in common, but rarely are the specifics of those unique tendencies identical.

In the end, these things matter most:
        How well did you love?
        How fully did you live?
        How deeply did you learn to let go?

                                —Jack Kornfield

MY COMMUNICATION PREFERENCES (Partner A)

These are my communication preferences for important or difficult conversations. Casual conversations do not need this level of awareness and planning. However, if casual conversations are getting problematic, having brainstorming and problem-solving conversations about your casual conversation effectiveness may be helpful.

Each person fills this out alone. Make a date to share the information with each other. You are not limited to these parameters. Add preferences as needed. *Remember, these are tools to use if you want to increase the likelihood of your partner hearing you and understanding you.*

Times of day that are good for me for an important conversation.

Preparation time I need before an important discussion.

Percolating time I need after hearing about an issue or topic.

This is how I prefer you use the sense of touch.

These are my preferred locations for important communication.

These are good words or phrases for me.

These are words or phrases to avoid.

Listen to yourself with still attention,
with spaciousness.

MY COMMUNICATION PREFERENCES (Partner B)

These are my communication preferences for important or difficult conversations. Casual conversations do not need this level of awareness and planning. However, if casual conversations are getting problematic, having brainstorming and problem-solving conversations about your casual conversation effectiveness may be helpful.

Each person fills this out alone. Make a date to share the information with each other. You are not limited to these parameters. Add preferences as needed. *Remember, these are tools to use if you want to increase the likelihood of your partner hearing you and understanding you.*

Times of day that are good for me for an important conversation.

Preparation time I need before an important discussion.

Percolating time I need after hearing about an issue or topic.

This is how I prefer you use the sense of touch.

These are my preferred locations for important communication.

These are good words or phrases for me.

These are words or phrases to avoid.

Listen to yourself with still attention,
with spaciousness.

OUR BLENDED COMMUNICATION PREFERENCES

CHANNELS THAT WORK

Fill this out together after sharing your individual channel preferences. This may need some brainstorming and negotiation.

Times of day on which we can compromise for important discussions.

Recommended preparation time before a discussion.

Recommended percolating time for each person, if needed.

This is how we will each use the sense of touch with the other. (The likelihood is the answer will not be the same for each person.)

These are our recommended locations for communication.

These are helpful words or phrases for each of us.

These are words or phrases to avoid using.

Understand your brain chemistry.
Understand your partner's brain
chemistry.

CHAPTER 9

CONVERSATION TYPES

This is a daily, if not hourly, needed skill set.

These four conversation types have some overlapping skill sets and very different goals. If you're each part of the same conversation, but not the same *type* of conversation, chances are you're having classic miscommunication without knowing why.

- Casual conversation
- Venting conversation
- Brainstorming conversation
- Problem-solving conversation

Here are brief descriptions of the four types of conversations and the tools needed for each type.

CASUAL CONVERSATION

Goal: A casual conversation is the two-way general exchange of daily information.

These are the most common conversations. Casual daily conversations are about coordinating current and reoccurring daily events.

Casual conversations that are not effective can add misunderstandings, inefficiency, and stress to everyday events. Over a very short time, these miscommunications will pile up and trigger annoyance, resentment, and even anger.

Casual conversations need these tools to be effective:

- Speak clearly
- Speak loud enough to be heard
- Use optimal tone and cadence
- Be in the same room together whenever possible
- Be facing each other or moving toward each other
- Make eye contact if possible
- Acknowledge each other in the exchange
- Check for understanding, if helpful

When you use these tools, there are fewer miscommunications and misunderstandings.

VENTING CONVERSATION

Goal: A venting conversation is for one person to let off steam about a situation. It is one-way emotional and informational sharing for the purpose of being heard and acknowledged.

Venting conversations are the most misunderstood. When one partner needs to gripe, complain, or let off steam about a situation with which she has unusually strong and mostly negative feelings, she wants to have a venting conversation.

Venting conversations are not casual, brainstorming, or problem-solving conversations. If you use brainstorming or problem-solving skills when someone is venting she will probably get angry (or angrier than she already is now) with you.

When someone needs to vent, she should be explicit. "I want to have a venting conversation. Are you available to listen to a venting conversation for ten minutes?" If, your partner says, "No, I am not available," then you need a plan B for yourself. Plan B means another person to vent with or another activity entirely, such as exercise, meditation, journaling, or all three.

GUIDELINES FOR THE SPEAKER AND THE LISTENER IN A VENTING CONVERSATION

For the PARTNER LISTENING AS ONE WHO CARES:

1. Listen. You have two ears and one mouth for this reason.
2. Without interrupting, use acknowledging words and behaviors to support your partner. You will have examples from your partner stating what acknowledging words and behaviors sound like and look like in her Venting Preferences.
3. Be aware of and use your partner's Venting Preferences.
4. Remember, this is about your partner. It's not about you. If she wants to vent about her job, or a situation with a coworker or a friend, your job is to listen to her description of the situation and her feelings about it.

Here is a partial list of what not to do.

    a. Don't offer suggestions to fix it

    b. Don't tell her how she is wrong

    c. Don't explain how it does not matter

    d. Don't interject what you did when it happened to you

    e. Don't say that it is her fault

    f. Don't get emotionally reactive, such as angry, defensive, or impatient

    g. Don't act inattentive; looking at your watch, doing something else while listening

    h. Don't interrupt

5. If your partner is venting about a situation involving you, this is where your partner gets to vehemently, yet respectfully, express and communicate her hurt, frustration, or anger (to name a few feelings) about a situation. The venting conversation is not about brainstorming or problem solving the issue.

6. If you're not in a good place to be a ***listener who cares***, respectfully say "No. I'm not available to support you in that way right now." If you will be available in five minutes, at 2:00 p.m., or tomorrow at breakfast, you may offer those times to your partner. ***Don't be a venting partner if you're not ready, or if the subject is too triggering for you. You may not be the appropriate venting partner in many situations.***

For the PARTNER WHO WANTS AND NEEDS TO VENT:

1. Specifically state, "I would like to have a venting conversation." Remember, this isn't a brainstorming or problem solving conversation. It is certainly not a casual conversation.

2. Say when you would like it to happen. Be specific. Now, in five minutes, at 2:00 p.m.

3. Ask if your partner is available and wants to participate as a ***listener who cares about you.*** "Are you available as a listener for a venting conversation?"

If he is not able to participate, accept his position and find another constructive way to take care of your self.

  a. Exercise, do something physical that is also constructive
  b. Journal
  c. Read something nurturing and grounding, such as prayer, poetry, or a daily thoughts book
  d. Use cathartic and soothing music
  e. Meditate
  f. Call a supportive person
  g. Have other potential venting partners

4. If your partner is willing and able to participate, limit yourself to ten minutes or less of venting. Use your venting preferences. Don't make personal attacks. Vent about a specific situation or a specific reoccurring situation.

5. The drama of name-calling, cursing, and sarcasm is too often used to emphasize dissatisfaction or anger. It will happen. However, in most cases it's not helpful and actually feeds the negativity of the situation. Find a less destructive way to express your negative emotions.

6. Take a deep breath or two before, during, and after venting.

7. End on a positive note. Thank your venting partner for the listening support. Let your partner know how he has been helpful. Express and show your appreciation as soon after venting as is comfortable and again within the next twenty-four hours when you feel calm or more positive.

8. If you think you'll need to vent again on the same issue, because it is recurring, it continues to build up, or there is just more to process, ask to reschedule another venting time.

Note: There is a gender issue here. Women are socialized more than men to notice and express emotions, therefore, women are more likely than men to identify the need to vent. Men are socialized from a very early age to roll with things, not be emotionally expressive, and suck it up and "be a man." As a result they are predisposed to not even identify the need to vent. Safe venting is an excellent skill for men and women to develop.

VENTING PREFERENCES (Partner A)

Fill this out at a time when you are calm and do not need to vent. Revisit your preferences and update them as needed. Share each update in writing with your partner.

What do you want from your partner when you have a venting conversation? How can he be a respectful and supportive *listener for you* when you are venting?

First, is your partner the appropriate person with whom to vent?

- On this subject?
- At this time?

Often he is not. It is helpful to have two or three venting resources. List two or three possible venting partners:

1.

2.

3.

Be specific in describing what you want from your partner. Describe what it would look like and sound like if you could observe yourself in a venting conversation with your partner being a supportive and attentive listener.

Positioning: Do you prefer sitting? Standing? Walking? Do you want your partner to be facing you or alongside you? Do you want to be at eye level with each other?

Proximity: How close or far do you want your partner to be while you vent? Does it change during the process?

Touch: Do you want your partner to touch you? When? Where? How? Does it change during the process? Do you want to be held in his arms? Hold hands? Not be touched at all? Wait until you are finished venting for touching? Do you want him to initiate touch or only respond when you initiate?

Eye Contact: How important is it to you? Does your partner know if you would like more or less eye contact? How will you let him know?

Acknowledgments That Work for You: Are there phrases you would prefer? Are there phrases to avoid? Be specific.

Understand your need to be heard
and acknowledged.

Understand your partner's need
to be heard and acknowledged.

VENTING PREFERENCES (Partner B)

Fill this out at a time when you are calm and do not need to vent. Revisit your preferences and update them as needed. Share each update in writing with your partner.

What do you want from your partner when you have a venting conversation? How can he be a respectful and supportive *listener for you* when you are venting?

First, is your partner the appropriate person with whom to vent?

- On this subject?
- At this time?

Often he is not. It is helpful to have two or three venting resources. List two or three possible venting partners:

1.

2.

3.

Be specific in describing what you want from your partner. Describe what it would look like and sound like if you could observe yourself in a venting conversation with your partner being a supportive and attentive listener.

Positioning: Do you prefer sitting? Standing? Walking? Do you want your partner to be facing you or alongside you? Do you want to be at eye level with each other?

Proximity: How close or far do you want your partner to be while you vent? Does it change during the process?

Touch: Do you want your partner to touch you? When? Where? How? Does it change during the process? Do you want to be held in his arms? Hold hands? Not be touched at all? Wait until you are finished venting for touching? Do you want him to initiate touch or only respond when you initiate?

Eye Contact: How important is it to you? Does your partner know if you would like more or less eye contact? How will you let him know?

Acknowledgments That Work for You: Are there phrases you would prefer? Are there phrases to avoid? Be specific.

Understand your need to be heard
and acknowledged.

Understand your partner's need
to be heard and acknowledged.

Brainstorming Conversation

Goal: A brainstorming conversation is to create ideas and options. This is a successful technique in business, research, and development. In a couple, it is a two-way expression of ideas for creating beneficial options to a situation.

Brainstorming conversations are for when you are exploring options. Where shall we go on vacation? Where do we want to move? What shall we do when my folks come to visit? How shall we divide household chores? How can we do a better job with our financial budget? How can we find more time for making love?

These are conversations where the goal is to create new ideas. In this kind of conversation, it's important to welcome new ideas, no matter how seemingly tangential. This isn't the time to judge the merits of the ideas, but rather to stir up the idea energy. After you have a minimum number of ideas (seven is strongly recommended as a minimum number in most cases), move on to the evaluating and problem-solving conversation.

When you brainstorm seven options, the most likely final solution will include combining aspects of a number of different options. For example, half of option two, part of seven and smidgen of option six. Problem solving with fewer options is likely to produce less resourceful results.

GUIDELINES FOR BRAINSTORMING CONVERSATIONS

1. Write one specific topic or issue to brainstorm.

2. Set a specific time and place for the brainstorming session.

3. Limit yourself to about forty-five minutes or less. Schedule a second session if you need more time.

4. Write down the parameters of the issue.

5. List the brainstorming ideas, hopefully seven or more.

6. Schedule a second brainstorming session, if needed, or schedule a problem-solving session.

Some couples know each other too well in againstness.

How do you learn to be with each other in collaboration?

BRAINSTORMING CONVERSATION SESSION
(Partner A)

Date and Time (limit to 45 minutes):

Place (supports calm and effectiveness):

Topic (only *one* topic):

Brainstorming Ideas:

1.

2.

3.

4.

5.

6.

7.

Some couples know each other too well
in againstness.

How do you learn to be with each other
in collaboration?

BRAINSTORMING CONVERSATION SESSION
(Partner B)

Date and Time (limit to 45 minutes):

Place (supports calm and effectiveness):

Topic (only *one* topic):

Brainstorming Ideas:

1.

2.

3.

4.

5.

6.

7.

You have to be open to knowing yourself
to have healthy relationships.

Problem-Solving Conversation

Goal: A problem-solving conversation is for exploring and weighing a number of options and making a decision. In a couple, it is a two-way shared process. Two heads are usually better than one. Each person gets to express his or her thoughts and feelings about the different possibilities. Each person gets to listen.

1. Set guidelines for how long each person will speak on the merits of an option. For example, we will each take two minutes to discuss the benefits and drawbacks of an option. After we have each made our initial comments we can take two more minutes each to address the option if either of us feel the need. Do this for each option. Some options may take very little time; others may go back and forth three or four times.

2. Rewrite and reorder the options after the first pass through the list. New ideas may have emerged, options may have been grouped together, and priorities may have been clarified or even changed. In many cases, this may be a very short process.

3. If you're in partial disagreement, list what you agree on and list where there is disagreement. List possible compromises.

4. If this issue is more significant to one person, the other person who finds the issue less significant can defer and earn cooperation credit for a difficult time in the future.

5. If there is still strong disagreement, you will eventually have to let one party's views and preferences take priority. Notice when this happens because you can take turns on who gets her way. Resentment is less likely to become part of the process if you take turns on not getting things your way. Additionally, you get feedback from the decision and its consequences. That additional data may give you important information for the next time the situation comes up.

6. Whatever the final decision is, summarize it in writing, and have both parties initial or sign the agreement. This is for clarity and consistency. Having written notes avoids many misunderstandings and arguments. We tend to remember things with filters that conveniently best suit ourselves. So, for the purposes of clarity and relational peace, put important or difficult decisions in writing.

How conflict is resolved
is directly related to how secure
you are in the relationship
and how secure you are in yourself.

PROBLEM-SOLVING CONVERSATION SESSION

Date and Time (limit to forty-five minutes):

Place (supports calm and effectiveness):

Topic (only *one* topic):

USE THE BRAINSTORMING WORKSHEET IDEAS.

How many minutes will each person have for her initial input?

How many minutes will be for discussion and evaluation between the parties?

Who will be the scribe for the summary (as referenced in Item No. 6 on the previous page)?

After initial input, discussion, and evaluation rewrite your updated version of your options if you have not already come to an agreement.

Again, take the time for input from each party, then discuss and evaluate. If you have not resolved how to deal with the issue, have you narrowed the choices? Are you moving in the right direction?

Do you need more information, more input, additional eyes, ears, and brains involved? Do you need to do more research?

Will you need to compromise? What will compromise look like? Who is more invested in the issue? Who is more experienced with the issue? Who will have to implement or carry out the decision? Who has a better track record with this type of issue?

Weigh all the contextual factors and come to a decision you are both willing to work toward. Verbally and nonverbally, acknowledge each other's input and support. Set up a time for review and follow-up. There's a lot of wisdom gained in the review process that will help the problem-solving process next time.

The ancestor of every action is a thought.

—Ralph Waldo Emerson

Summary of Four Kinds of Conversations

- Casual conversation—two way general exchange of daily information

- Venting conversation—one way emotional sharing for acknowledgment

- Brainstorming conversation—two way creating idea energy

- Problem-solving conversation—two way prioritizing and deciding

Are you both clear about what kind of conversation you are having?
Are you using the appropriate skills for the conversation?

Summary

Breathe

10 ESSENTIAL COMMUNICATION

This is a daily needed skill set.

If you do not have the skills to fight fair and constructively with each other, this needs to be a daily practice of awareness and intention until you have the skills.

- Learn how to fight with each other
- Learn how to express and work through hurt
- Learn how to express and work through anger
- Learn how to express and work through disagreement
- Learn how to self-soothe

Are you are aware that communication skills are vital for healthy couples? If you do not have these skills and you are not trying to acquire these skills, you are choosing to live in a more difficult relationship.

Your family of origin may have left you wanting in the skill area of disagreement, anger, hurt, and self-soothing. It is common for people in the communication and helping fields to have stories about coming out of environments where there was a need for more respectful and effective communication and conflict skills in their homes while growing up. This is a great opportunity. You can now develop these skills with the wisdom and deliberateness of an adult. This is a very powerful place to be.

Or, your family of origin tried very hard to teach you these skills and you just needed some more lessons. And, if this is the case, congratulations, if you are reading this now and you apply yourself to this issue you will find many priceless rewards.

There should be zero tolerance for hurtful and harmful fighting words and behaviors. Zero tolerance means if hurtful and harmful words and behaviors happen (and they will), you address them with thoughtful immediacy. If they are not addressed with amends, learning, and repairs, the relationship will likely deteriorate at an accelerated rate if you are lucky. If you are not so lucky, you may be in this miserable pattern for 5, 10, 20 years.

BEHAVIORS AND WORDS THAT DO NOT WORK

1. Starting the conversation with harsh words and a harsh tone. It will only get worse from there

2. Being too intense in tone, word, or volume

3. Name-calling

4. Cursing

5. Using sarcasm

6. Blaming

7. Negative labeling, such as "You are hopeless."

8. Using black and white thinking and language (one person is all wrong and the other is all right)

9. Using the words *always* and *never* as in "You always have to have the last word" or "You never say 'I'm sorry.'"

10. Ignoring

11. Belittling

12. Minimizing

13. Being the expert and/or the judge over your partner (even if you are the expert)

14. Mind reading (telling your partner what he thinks or feels)

15. Garbage bagging: Not staying in the present moment with the present situation, but having a long list of past grievances (some that are years old) and hurts that you bring out each time you are angry. You may want to research forgiveness on the internet.

16. Having a Venting Conversation without letting your partner know that this is what you need and want and not allowing him to participate in the process. See Types of Conversations, Chapter 9.

17. Ambushing your partner when he is not ready

18. Talking without a pause

19. Talking over your partner

20. Intimidating language, volume, tone, or body language

21. Physical intimidation of any kind, such as looming over the other, threatening gestures, throwing things, hitting things, slamming doors

22. Threatening harm to yourself or others

23. Threatening to damage things

24. Threatening to withhold affection or support

25. Not remembering HALTS – not communicating on anything difficult when either of you are Hungry, Angry, Late, Tired or Sick

Add to this list on your own.

A significant issue, which commonly occurs when an adult develops new awareness of how poorly he has communicated with those people whom he cares about the most, is the issue of shame. This is an issue for both men and women; however in heterosexual couples the issue is more common with men. He is emotionally devastated and ashamed when he realizes how much he has hurt his loved ones. If you choose to become stuck here, with shame as your emotional companion, you will again be hurting yourself and those close to you.

The important point to remember is you are not responsible for what you did not know in the past. However, you are responsible as soon as you do know. As soon as you realize you are unnecessarily hurting yourself or another:

- Stop and breathe.
- Take a few seconds or minutes to slow down.
- Make a more balanced choice in your tone, words, or behavior.
- Take a time-out. Count to one hundred slowly.
- Get support. Ask for help.
- Take time to connect and make repairs with yourself, your partner, and your family.

Choose repairs over feeling sorry for yourself. Let yourself grieve the loss of your illusion of being righteous. Then celebrate that awareness because it is a blessing of a realization, and now move with a more spacious heart, meaning with more compassion for yourself and others.

BEHAVIORS AND WORDS THAT FACILITATE CONNECTION, EVEN IN STRONG DISAGREEMENT

1. Use the necessary verbal and nonverbal communication elements in Chapter 7.

2. Use your partner's channels that work in Chapter 8.

3. Use HALTS.

4. Take a time-out if either of you is too escalated, 6.5 or above on a scale of 0 to 10 (Nonverbal Skill 1 in Chapter 7, Setting the Stage).

5. Take a deep breath to calm yourself. Be aware of your breathing during the communication process. Use your breath, posture, and words to support calmness.

6. Be assertive. Check if you are coming across assertively. If you are aggressive take a time-out, and when you are ready, attend to Nonverbal Skill 1, setting the stage for calmness and respect.

7. Stick to one topic.
   Note: In Items 8, 9, and 10, the points made in the sub-items for "a" are related to one story, those for "b" are related to a second story, and those for "c" are related to a third story.

8. Use "I messages" and feeling words, (See Appendix A: Feelings List) such as:

   a. I am angry.

   b. I am hurt.

   c. I feel taken for granted.

9. Be more specific with your "I" messages and feeling words (describing the behavior which invites the feeling):

   a. I am angry because we are an hour late for our engagement.

   b. I am hurt when you do not make time for our love life.

   c. I feel taken for granted when we do not take the opportunity to go out on a date alone, just the two of us.

10. Suggest a remedy to the complaint in three or four sentences.

    a. Call me as soon as you know you will be late. Keep me in

the loop. Even if you are late because of rush hour traffic, you can let me know. *Pause for acknowledgment.*

b. If you're not able to let me know, would you acknowledge the lateness and your awareness of its difficulty on me when you first arrive? *Pause for acknowledgment.*

c. I would like us to prioritize our love life by planning our week together every Sunday afternoon after lunch between 1:00 and 2:00 p.m. Can we start next Sunday?

11. Ask your partner about her feelings and thoughts about the situation.

12. Ask your partner about her thoughts on a remedy for the situation.

13. Agree on a solution together. Include things <u>each</u> of you can <u>do</u> to keep this pattern from recurring.

14. Set aside a follow up time (over the weekend, one week, two weeks, a month) to revisit the issue. Notice, reiterate, keep the behaviors that have worked, and brainstorm adjustments to the behaviors that have not worked or not improved enough. **This is critical. To highlight, to pay attention to the behaviors you want to keep. We tend to give more attention to what we do not want, the negative behaviors. That emotional and verbal stance actually adds fuel and focus to the problem rather than the solutions.**

15. Thank your partner for listening, caring, and brainstorming. Ask your partner if your communication in this case felt respectful and clear for her. Reiterate your appreciation for her working on communication patterns with you even with difficult issues. Ask if you could have shared your thoughts and feelings in a better way for her.

SHARE YOUR COMMUNICATION HISTORY

At various times of smooth communication, discuss your communication histories with each other. If this is not appropriate to do with your partner right now, start with a therapist, support group, or appropriate friend. Working with another on your communication history should not be a secret from your partner (unless power, control, or violence is an issue). You should update him as you grow in insight.

What did communication look like, sound like and feel like in your family of origin? Who were your models and mentors in communication? Use these questions as a starting place for a series of fifteen-minute discussions on your communication history.

1. What are specific examples of respectful communication?

2. What are specific examples of disrespectful communication?

3. What are three or four of your worst memories around communication?

4. What were unspoken rules around communication? Such as:

   • "We do not deal with uncomfortable feelings directly." This kind of rule is commonly not discussed or passed on in words. If you grow up in a family with this rule, you have a double bind. You cannot talk about the unspoken rule that you cannot talk about certain feelings.

   • "Who gets the last word?

   • "Who has dibs on the truth?"

   • "Don't upset (Dad)."

   • "Don't tell (Mom)."

   • "Children are to be seen and not heard."

   • "Whatever the kids want, the kids get."

5. What have been some challenging communication circumstances?

6. What did you learn from the experiences?

7. How were positive feelings expressed in your family of origin?

8. How were negative feelings expressed in your family of origin?

9. How were differences expressed and processed in your family of origin?

10. Who have been communication role models for each of you?

11. What are each of your communication strengths?

12. What are your communication goals as a couple and individually?

Discussing these historical patterns in each of your families of origin allows you to make informed choices on:

- What patterns would you like to perpetuate and nurture in your couple relationship?

- What patterns would you like to replace either partially or entirely?

- What new patterns do you want to add?

You may need professional support in changing difficult and hurtful patterns. Professional help does not have to be expensive financially (it can be in a group or a class coupled with individual work) to be effective, but it does require work and a time commitment of months and years. It is worth it.

IF YOU EXPERIENCE A FIGHTING DISASTER: UNCONTROLLED HOSTILE WORDS AND/OR BEHAVIORS

If you have a "disaster of a fight" that was not respectful, not productive, left both of you more angry and hurt and feeling drained, and possibly hopeless or stuck, there are lessons to be learned and repairs to be made.

Fill out Worksheet 10.1, Incident Report, after any problematic communication event to analyze what you can change about the circumstances in order to achieve a less painful outcome.

Learn how to make repairs. Gottman's research stresses the importance of learning how to make repairs. Repairs are an important set of tools after a fight. Repairs are to articulate and demonstrate:

1. Care and connection

2. What you have learned

3. What you are sorry for

4. What you appreciate about your partner

5. What you appreciate about the relationship

6. What you can do together and separately to change the negative pattern

Repairs include:

1. Sincere apologies in a manner that works for the receiver of the apology

2. Acknowledgment of what your partner felt

3. Acknowledgment of your partner's views

4. Taking responsibility for what you did and or said which was not helpful

5. Devising a way together, to hit the reset button on a conversation that is not working well, such as "Can we have a reset?" "Can we have a take two?" or "Can we have a do-over?"

6. Verbally and physically appreciating that your partner is working with you on effective and respectful communication

7. Agreeing to address the issue sooner, before it gets intense

8. Letting your partner know what you learned and how you will address a similar situation differently next opportunity

9. Agreeing to both call and observe a time-out sooner

10. Agreeing to a time-out signal if words are a problem, the professional athlete's hands in a capital T is a great time-out signal

11. Using humor, *if it is shared humor*. Sarcasm or teasing, humor at the expense of another is destructive. If you have incompatible humor styles recognize that complication. You will need to brainstorm and problem solve that topic.

12. Appropriate use of touch, tone, and eye contact can significantly contribute to repair effectiveness (What works for your partner?)

13. Agreeing to listen attentively to your partner and have a specific plan on how to do that (nonverbal communication skills, Chapter 7)

Add repairs to this list as you discover them

WORKSHEET

INCIDENT REPORT

PROBLEMATIC COMMUNICATION EVENT

Each of you fills out this form individually. As soon as both of you are ready to revisit the Problematic Communication Event, schedule a Problematic Communication Event Autopsy. Then devise pattern interrupters and counter measures to the problematic pattern. The plan should specifically describe how to deal more effectively with the problems in 1) these specific circumstances, and possibly 2) generally related ones.

Date of Incident:

Time Started: Time Stopped:

Location:

In your view, how stressed were each of you before the event?

Party A	High	Medium High	Medium Low	Low
Party B	High	Medium High	Medium Low	Low

In your view, how stressed were each of you during the event?

Party A	High	Medium High	Medium Low	Low
Party B	High	Medium High	Medium Low	Low

In your view, how stressed were each of you after the event?

Party A	High	Medium High	Medium Low	Low
Party B	High	Medium High	Medium Low	Low

In your view, how stressed are each of you about this event, now?

Party A	High	Medium High	Medium Low	Low
Party B	High	Medium High	Medium Low	Low

Were there any major physical, physiological, or psychological complications at the time of the incident? (i.e., HALTS)

Who noticed the issue first?

How was the issue introduced?

What was said or done well?

What would you do or say differently if you could turn back the hands of time and redo the event with the wisdom you have now? Would you set the stage in a different way? Pick a different time? Listen more? Talk less? Breathe more? Exercise first? Give or take more Percolating Time?

Has anything good come out of the incident?

What repairs would be helpful for each of you now?

INCIDENT REPORT, FOLLOW-UP (Partner A)

PROBLEMATIC COMMUNICATION EVENT AUTOPSY

Fill out this second form within a week of Worksheet 10.1. Fill out this form separately or together. If you fill it out separately, make a date to share your thoughts with each other.

1. Notice what has worked or feels better, or is moving in the right direction. Describe in detail.

2. Notice what you would like to see continue. Describe in detail.

3. What words or behaviors would you like to have more of? Be specific and describe in detail.

4. What would you like to change (small and doable) about your behaviors? Be specific and describe in detail.

ISSUE	REPAIR
1.	
2.	
3.	

5. Notice what would be better to process with a third party. Schedule a date and wait until that time.

Remember you have choice
in each moment.

WORKSHEET

INCIDENT REPORT, FOLLOW-UP (Partner B)

PROBLEMATIC COMMUNICATION EVENT AUTOPSY

Fill out this second form within a week of Worksheet 10.1. Fill out this form separately or together. If you fill it out separately, make a date to share your thoughts with each other.

1. Notice what has worked or feels better, or is moving in the right direction. Describe in detail.

2. Notice what you would like to see continue. Describe in detail.

3. What words or behaviors would you like to have more of? Be specific and describe in detail.

4. What would you like to change (small and doable) about your behaviors? Be specific and describe in detail.

ISSUE	REPAIR
1.	
2.	
3.	

5. Notice what would be better to process with a third party. Schedule a date and wait until that time.

Remember you have choice
in each moment.

CHAPTER 11

THE IMPORTANCE OF BALANCE BASICS

This is a daily needed skill.

Balance awareness sells itself.

> *If you practice balance awareness*
> *life tends to flow*
> *rather than grind.*

Balance awareness consists of self-care, couple care, and family care along with meeting the needs of the outside world such as jobs, bills, paperwork, and so on.

Too frequently, people use the squeaky wheel approach to life; that which is most pressing and most demanding gets the time and attention. In most cases, the demands of the outside world consisting of work, community and extended family are the loudest and most public and they get the bulk of your life energy.

You and your partner and family get the leftovers.

Unfortunately, the family and couple needs are too often addressed with the same squeaky wheel approach.

So feeling not enough, behind, and overwhelmed can become a sad choice of lifestyle.

Even if you participate in one part of your life extremely well, such as work, it is often not as rewarding if the rest of your life is out of balance and not working well.

Balance awareness requires that you prioritize your time and energy when it comes to self-care, couple care, and family care.

It is important not to frame these as competing needs. Instead, view them as co-occurring systemic needs.

Our relational systems operate similarly to our biological systems. For smooth functioning, the body needs many different elements in certain proportions (i.e., vitamins, proteins, carbohydrates, fats). Further, any subsystem imbalance in the body over time, as in relationships, takes a toll on the whole system.

Relational systems, similar to body systems, can repair and recover even after being damaged, neglected, or stressed for a very long time. The next several chapters cover awareness of needs and techniques for evaluating and adjusting your life balance.

There needs to be a plan to meet the co-occurring needs of the individuals in the relationship, the couple, and the family. You have to be aware of the balance deficits, indulgences, and trajectories and make the necessary periodic course adjustments.

Don't wait for the rest of the world to make room for your personal care, couple time, and family time because that won't happen. You and your partner have the power to improve the balance in your couples relationship and your lives.

You and your partner are responsible for balance awareness, separately and together.

BALANCE BASICS OVERVIEW

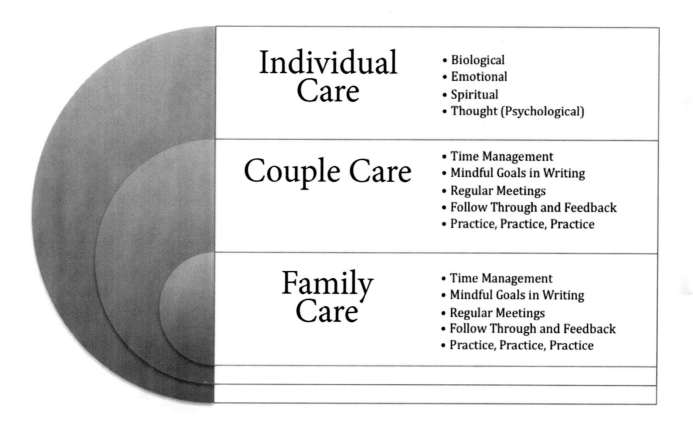

Individual Care	• Biological • Emotional • Spiritual • Thought (Psychological)
Couple Care	• Time Management • Mindful Goals in Writing • Regular Meetings • Follow Through and Feedback • Practice, Practice, Practice
Family Care	• Time Management • Mindful Goals in Writing • Regular Meetings • Follow Through and Feedback • Practice, Practice, Practice

Take care of your body.
It's the only place you have
to live.

—Jim Rohn

SELF-CARE ESSENTIALS

This is a daily needed skill set.

Do your **B-E-S-T** for yourself, your partner, your family, and your community:

Biological

Emotional

Spirit(ual)

Thoughts

BIOLOGICAL HEALTH

If someone wanted to impair your functioning quickly, they could deprive you of an adequate amount of sleep, water, nutrition, exercise, fresh air, and sunshine. Diminishing these resources below a basic level leads to a decline in overall functioning. Diminishing these resources below a basic level is the opposite of ergonomics on all five criteria. It is less safe, less comfortable, it is harder to function, performance is impaired, and aesthetically it moves you away from balance and harmony.

Both short- and long-term imbalances can weaken an immune system, negatively effect mood and mood regulation, and impair thinking.

In our materially abundant culture, we regularly deprive ourselves of adequate amounts of these basic needs. We can artificially cover our imbalances with substances such as caffeine, nicotine, and alcohol, often for a long time. Eventually it takes a toll on our health.

Long before the health crisis though, there will be relational costs. When we are physically out of balance, we tend to take it out on those close to us.

Attending to basic health needs
is an individual,
couple, and family issue.

These are the basics for doing your biological best:

1. Sleep—Most adults need five 90-minute REM cycles a night, 7.5 to 8 hours a night. For more information on sleep, see the Mayo Clinic Website article, "Sleep guidelines: How many hours of sleep are enough?" at http://www.mayoclinic.com/health/how-many-hours-of-sleep-are-enough.

2. Hydration—Check with a nutritionist or dietician as to your personal requirements. A general guideline is approximately eight glasses of water a day. For more information see the Mayo Clinic Website article, "Water: How Much Should You Drink Every Day?" at http://www.mayoclinic.com/health/water.

3. Nutrition—Whole grains, vegetables, fruits, lean protein, and healthy fats are important parts of healthy nutrition. For more information contact The American Dietetic Association at http://www.eatright.org.

4. Exercise—Walk, dance, bike, workout, and stretch the equivalent of 8,000 steps a day. Are you moving ninety minutes a day? For more information see the Mayo Clinic Website article, "Exercise: 7 Benefits of Regular Physical Activity: Need Motivation to Exercise? Here Are Seven Ways Exercise Can Improve Your Life—Starting Today!" at http://www.mayoclinic.com/health/exercise.

5. Fresh Air, Oxygen—Learn about and practice proper breathing at http://www.drweil.com/drw/u/ART00521/three-breathing-exercises.html or http://www.stop-anxiety-attack-symptoms-com. And if this seems absurd to you, you surely need the information.

6. Sunlight—A minimum of thirty minutes a day of direct natural light is important for health and a sense of well-being. (Note: 4, 5, and 6 can be accomplished together.)

Biological care is a to-do list and a general guide. We each need to make adjustments for our individual requirements. On a regular basis, situations may cause temporary imbalances. **Regularly evaluating your biological needs and the situational stressors is important to the long-term health of your body and your relationships.**

Your body is a temple,
but only if you treat it as one.
— Astrid Alauda

BASIC BIOLOGIC NEED	COMMON SHORT TERM IMBALANCE COMPLICATIONS
SLEEP	Irritability Weaker Immune System Fatigue Weight Gain Poorer Response Time Poorer Decision Making
HYDRATION	Irritability Weaker Immune System Fatigue Weight Gain Poorer Response Time Poorer Decision Making
NUTRITION	Irritability Weaker Immune System Fatigue Weight Gain or Loss Poorer Response Time Poorer Decision Making Impaired Sleep
EXERCISE	Irritability Weaker Immune System Fatigue Weight Gain Poorer Response Time Poorer Decision Making Impaired Sleep
FRESH AIR	Irritability Moodiness Depression Impaired Sleep
SUNLIGHT	Irritability Moodiness Depression Impaired Sleep

Get the picture?

Additionally, if you have any health complications such as anxiety, depression, stressful job, blood pressure issues, diabetic issues, or weakened immune system issues, then these basics are even more important to address.

The long-term complications of imbalances are worse.

Wherever you are right now in this process of awareness and health, don't give up. People in far worse circumstances have made marked improvements and so can you.

You can develop a plan. Use worksheet 12.1

WORKSHEET

BALANCE INVENTORY (Partner A)

INDIVIDUAL SELF-CARE: BIOLOGICAL ASSESSMENT AND PLAN FOR IMPROVEMENT

On a scale of 1 to 5:

1 = very poor
2 = somewhat poor
3 = mostly adequate
4 = very adequate
5 = excellent, this is not a problem

Mark in one color where you presently are in these areas of biological self-care. Then in a different color mark where you want to be in the next week or month. Make it a realistic and doable goal.

Sleep	1	2	3	4	5
Hydration	1	2	3	4	5
Nutrition	1	2	3	4	5
Exercise	1	2	3	4	5
Fresh Air	1	2	3	4	5
Sunlight	1	2	3	4	5

How will you achieve your goals? Specifically describe what you'll do differently and when.

Once you are clear with your behavioral goals, put them on your calendar. Be sure to plan for addressing setbacks and resets. Keep coming back to your written plan. Brainstorm replacement behaviors for any recurring setbacks. Include your partner and your support network in your planning. Describe your behavioral goals in specifics in writing. Reuse worksheet 12.1 as needed. If you forget or get off track (and you will,) it takes a few minutes to regroup and recommit to your self-care plans.

Balance is a dynamic process of many overlapping alternations.

—Deng Ming-Dao

12.1

BALANCE INVENTORY (Partner B)

INDIVIDUAL SELF-CARE: BIOLOGICAL ASSESSMENT AND PLAN FOR IMPROVEMENT

On a scale of 1 to 5:

>   1 = very poor
>   2 = somewhat poor
>   3 = mostly adequate
>   4 = very adequate
>   5 = excellent, this is not a problem

Mark in one color where you presently are in these areas of biological self-care. Then in a different color mark where you want to be in the next week or month. Make it a realistic and doable goal.

Sleep	1	2	3	4	5
Hydration	1	2	3	4	5
Nutrition	1	2	3	4	5
Exercise	1	2	3	4	5
Fresh Air	1	2	3	4	5
Sunlight	1	2	3	4	5

How will you achieve your goals? Specifically describe what you'll do differently and when.

Once you are clear with your behavioral goals, put them on your calendar. Be sure to plan for setbacks and resets. Keep coming back to your written plan. Brainstorm replacement behaviors for any recurring setbacks. Include your partner and your support network in your planning. Describe your behavioral goals in specifics in writing. Reuse worksheet 12.1 as needed. If you forget or get off track (and you will,) it takes a few minutes to regroup and recommit to your self-care plans.

Balance is a dynamic process of
many overlapping alternations.

—Deng Ming-Dao

EMOTIONAL HEALTH

Emotional wellness exists in a community. Emotional wellness consists of noticing your feelings and choosing healthy behaviors. Emotional wellness is also noticing the feelings of others and choosing healthy behaviors.

We all need social activity that is positive. This means behavior that is relatively safe and stimulating for your brain, body, and spirit that takes place in a variety of circumstances. It can be a walk in a park with your partner, a bike ride alone, dancing with friends, jamming with a band, or playing card games. Blending these diverse aspects is the art of living. You will need some mixture of the following.

These are the basics for doing your emotional best:

1. Activity that is positive alone.

   Reading • Exercise • Meditation • Writing • Biking • Walking

2. Social activity that is positive as a couple with others.

   Dancing • Book Group • Bar-B-Q • Games • Music • Hiking

3. Social activity that is positive alone, as a couple.

   Massage • Cooking •Walking • Games • Pet Time • Reading

4. Social activity that is positive individually with others.

   Music • Volunteering • Sports • Exercise • Classes • Book Groups

5. Social activity that is positive as a family with others.

   Picnic • Sports • Theatre • Music • Community Events • Holidays

6. Social activity that is positive alone, as a family.

   Travel • Holidays • Hiking • Biking • Games • Theatre • Sports

7. Noticing your own feelings and acknowledging the feelings of others.

Are you aware of your feelings? This means, generally, at any specific time, can you identify what you are feeling and where you are feeling it in your body? Do you have more than three or four answers?

Do you have difficulty appropriately sharing what you are feeling with someone close to you? Do you have difficulty empathizing with what another may be feeling? Does the expression of certain feelings, words, or behaviors trigger you to withdraw or feel a need to protect yourself? If you have a strong "yes" to any of these questions, then chances are you need to learn to recognize, communicate about, and appropriately share your feelings. Furthermore, you need to be able to listen to another, specifically your partner, authentically discuss his feelings.

Here are two helpful ways to think about feelings:

1. Feelings are like a rainbow. You have a wide spectrum of feelings. Unacknowledged feelings tend to channel energy into your acceptable or habitual emotional states. If you suppress feelings, you tend to impair their quality of information and your life.

Occasionally, when I initially work with people, their emotional vocabulary is limited to three or four feelings such as happy, frustrated, OK, and annoyed. Everyone has a wide range of feelings, however it's common for people to lack the words and the body awareness needed to effectively process and work through emotions. See Appendix A for a list of feeling words.

Are there people in whose presence you are emotionally more skilled or less skilled? A classic example is people who emotionally function differently from their "norm" when their parents or authority figures are present.

Our socialization is to mask many of our feelings. We even mask them from ourselves.

Learning about what you are feeling and knowing that you do not have to be a victim of what you are feeling is a liberating growth experience.

All feelings are OK. Feelings are. You get to notice them.

How you behave when you have a feeling, what you do when you have a feeling, is another story.

Noticing feelings is not the same as letting them create a soap opera of havoc or take you on an emotional or relational roller coaster ride. Feelings should provide information, not run your life.

Feelings provide information about:

- What you like and do not like
- What you want more of
- What you want less of
- Unhealed loss and pain from the past
- What you do not want to expose yourself to
- Where you need to do some personal work
- A sense of connection, when you share feelings with another and she shares her feelings with you

2. Feelings are like clouds. You get to notice them as they pass by. Again, you have a wide range of choices of how to behave when feelings occur.

If you're angry and you express it without hesitation, you may hurt someone close to you, someone you love and care about very much. If you express it without hesitation in a public place, to a stranger, you may find yourself at a minimum being questioned by security personnel.

However, if you take your angry feelings and choose to work them out of your system with exercise, physical chores, artistic expression, or stretching, you get very different results. People with physical limitations can use stretching, talking to a friend, and listening to music to work the negative feeling energy out of their bodies.

Negative feelings have a brain and body chemistry that is best expressed or processed by being physical. You have the choice whether the physical behavior you choose is constructive or destructive.

You are not limited to the behavioral choices you have made in the past around your feelings. You can train yourself to acknowledge what feelings you are experiencing, and to make personally and socially beneficial behavioral choices around those same feelings. You can have a plan of action, rather than live in helpless reaction.

HOW TO LEARN ABOUT YOUR FEELINGS

Children's Books

Good children's books represent the essence of what is important. They are simple in their words, yet philosophically and psychologically complex.

Quality children's books express and explain life in nurturing ways. Authors of children's books are not afraid of difficult topics. There are excellent children's books about work, travel, feelings, imagination, science, and nature. Additionally, there are wonderful and beautiful children's books about pain, cancer, loss, divorce, and death.

Reading to a child is a wonderful way to learn about feelings. The book can be a catalyst, and experiencing it with a child is to be at the elbow of a great teacher. If you have young children in your life that are not your daily responsibility (nieces and nephews, godchildren, neighbors' children), set aside time weekly or bi-monthly to read with them. It may only be fifteen minutes every week or two. With six months to a year of consistency, it benefits everyone involved, you, the child, the child's parents, the community, and your relationships. If you have young children as a daily responsibility, then, for both your benefit and their benefit, you should be reading to them daily.

Talk about your reading-with-kids experiences with your partner, family, and friends. Specifically, discuss what you are noticing about feelings.

See the Resource Section for a beginning list of recommended children's books.

Using Movies for Emotional Perspective and Growth

There is a reference book *Rent Two Films and Let's Talk in the Morning: Using Popular Movies in Psychotherapy* by John Hesley that references movies by situational and personal growth topics.

See the Resource Section for a list of recommended movies.

FEELING EXERCISES YOU CAN DO ALONE

This is a practical and easy way to learn about your feelings. Simply take a slow deep breath and ask yourself, "What am I feeling right now?" Ask yourself this question twenty times a day. It takes less than a minute to notice and describe in your mind what you feel in your body. Describe the body sensations to yourself. Then give the feeling a name. Notice what experiences or thoughts occurred prior to this feeling. If you do this ten, twenty, or thirty times a day for a month you can learn quite a bit about yourself and your feelings. See Appendix A, *A Feeling List*.

A second exercise takes a more formal time commitment. You can practice it in a number of different ways. Pick seven feelings, one for each day of the week. On each day of the week for a month, write (or meditate, or do something creative such as art, poetry, dance) about one feeling for five to seven minutes. Notice and learn about that one feeling four separate times in one month.

- How it registers in your body
- Recent experiences you have had with that feeling
- How that feeling has affected your life
- How it affects your relationships
- Write about your earliest memories of having that feeling
- Write about your strongest memories of that feeling
- Write about what it is like to experience your partner having that feeling or sharing that feeling with you
- Write about how you share that feeling with your parner

You can learn about your relationship with that feeling and how it has influenced your life and your worldview.

- What does it cost in time, energy, and money?
- Has it energized your life?
- Does it enrich your life?

A variation on this assignment is to pick fourteen feelings and write about each four times in two months. You can pick any number of feelings for any number of days. Have at least three or four opportunities to explore each feeling.

After you learn about your history with your feelings, you can morph the exercise into brainstorming how you would like to behave when you experience a particular feeling. What would you like to do and say when you experience this feeling? Is there a different habit or response you'd like to learn to have with a specific feeling? If you don't know behavioral options, look to mentors and what behaviors they model with their feelings. Mentors may be real people you know, people in leadership, people in history, or inspirational characters in books or movies.

Examples:

- Some Christians wear bracelets with "WWJD?" printed on them (What would Jesus do?) to remind them of behavioral choices.

- People have mentors in parents, grandparents, aunts, and uncles, and they carry an internal awareness, knowing when they're stuck or lost, to ask themselves "What would Grandma want for me?" or "How would Uncle Joe have dealt with this?"

- People look to teachers, supervisors, coaches, neighbors, or friends.

- People look to others in history whose lives they are familiar with, such as Gandhi, Martin Luther King, Eleanor Roosevelt, or Betty Ford.

- People look to created characters in books such as Atticus Finch in *To Kill A Mockingbird* or Celie in *The Color Purple*.

FEELING EXERCISES YOU CAN DO WITH YOUR PARTNER

Write six feelings on six different index cards. I recommend four of them be "positive" feelings and two of them be "challenging" feelings. Shuffle the cards and each person gets to take a fifteen-minute turn going through all twelve feeling cards and sharing whatever he wants to share about that feeling. The other party gets to *listen attentively* to his partner.

As you come to a feeling card, tell your partner something about what it is like for you when you experience this feeling. What invites this feeling to manifest? Say something like the following:

- I feel (fill in with the feeling on the card) when (xyz) happens.

- I remember feeling (state the feeling) when (xyz) happened.

- When I experience (feeling) this is how it registers in my body.

- These are the thoughts which go with (feeling).

- These are the memories that go with (feeling).

Do this exercise with regularity, weekly, bi-weekly, or monthly. Give your partner your full attention while he discusses his feelings. Learn about each other. Be present for each other. You may have to do this awkwardly a few times before you get comfortable with the process.

This is part of what "to honor each other" means.

If you're both already comfortable talking about your feelings, the above partner exercise may be a playful experience. When there are feelings that are more challenging to share and discuss, the exercise will be a growing experience. I find I learn about my partner of thirty-plus years anytime we do this exercise as an after dinner discussion.

You can also do the "brainstorming new habits with feelings" as a partner exercise. In this case, the partner gets to *listen*, unless specifically invited to brainstorm.

JOIN A PERSONAL GROWTH GROUP OR A SUPPORT GROUP

Learning about your feelings is similar to learning to play a musical instrument or learning to dance; with practice, you will benefit from the skill for the rest of your life. Some people make the expression and sharing of feelings a living art form. Some people touch our lives deeply by being good listeners.

Feelings come and go like clouds
in a windy sky.

—Thich Nhat Hanh

BALANCE INVENTORY (Partner A)

INDIVIDUAL SELF-CARE: EMOTIONAL FUNCTIONING ASSESSMENT AND PLAN FOR GROWTH

Using the words from the Feelings List in Appendix A as a reference, mark in one color where you presently are in an area of emotional awareness. In a different color mark where you want to be in the next week or month (make it a realistic and doable goal). Aim for solid growth through small specific behavioral steps.

On a scale of 1 to 5:

    1 = very poor
    2 = somewhat poor
    3 = mostly adequate
    4 = very adequate
    5 = excellent, this is not a problem

Circle the numbers that best describe your emotional skill level and goal level during __less__ stressful times:

Verbal Feeling Awareness	1	2	3	4	5
Body Feeling Awareness	1	2	3	4	5

Now do the same evaluation of your skills and goals during __more__ stressful times:

Verbal Feeling Awareness	1	2	3	4	5
Body Feeling Awareness	1	2	3	4	5

Are you behaviorally destructive with particular emotions? This means overdoing or unmindfully doing a behavior when certain emotions or intensity of emotion occurs. Examples of daily behaviors that can be practiced in destructive ways are to eat, spend money, use mind or mood altering substances (alcohol, tobacco, caffeine, prescription, or recreational substances), or demonstrate behaviors in an addictive manner (gamble, rage, drink, etc.) or in an unhealthy manner.

These destructive behaviors can accompany "positive" as well as "negative" emotions. Many people overspend or overindulge in alcohol or food when they are happy and celebrating.

List problematic behaviors and what emotions those behaviors are paired with.

1.

2.

3.

4.

5.

Now list what you can behaviorally do, in each case, to make the emotion have less of a problematic pattern.

1.

2.

3.

4.

5.

Does your partner express that you identify and articulate your feelings clearly? Ask him now and circle the number that best represents his response.

1   2   3   4   5

From your partner's feedback, what small behavior will you do differently around what feeling? State the feeling and the specific behavior.

Are you able to identify and express your emotions in a timely manner? Where are you and where would you like to be?

1   2   3   4   5

Some people are able to identify emotions better in retrospect and are less skilled in the present moment. This would be something to brainstorm, how to effectively process feelings in a timely manner. Strong emotional situations may need a time-out (meaning a let it go for a period of time or for an appropriate setting) or percolating time, both of which would need to be communicated respectfully.

What will you do and/or say when you have emotions occurring in a stressful situation?

How skilled are you at listening to your partner share her feelings? Where would you like to be?

1   2   3   4   5

Specifically, what three things can you do differently to be a better listener with your partner?

1.

2.

3.

Feelings come and go like clouds
in a windy sky.

—Thich Nhat Hanh

12.2

BALANCE INVENTORY (Partner B)

INDIVIDUAL SELF-CARE: EMOTIONAL FUNCTIONING ASSESSMENT AND PLAN FOR GROWTH

Using the words from the Feelings List in Appendix A as a reference, mark in one color where you presently are in an area of emotional awareness. In a different color mark where you want to be in the next week or month (make it a realistic and doable goal). Aim for solid growth through small specific behavioral steps.

On a scale of 1 to 5:

> 1 = very poor
> 2 = somewhat poor
> 3 = mostly adequate
> 4 = very adequate
> 5 = excellent, this is not a problem

Circle the numbers that best describe your emotional skill level and goal level during <u>less</u> stressful times:

Verbal Feeling Awareness	1	2	3	4	5
Body Feeling Awareness	1	2	3	4	5

Now do the same evaluation of your skills and goals during <u>more</u> stressful times:

Verbal Feeling Awareness	1	2	3	4	5
Body Feeling Awareness	1	2	3	4	5

Are you behaviorally destructive with particular emotions? This means overdoing or unmindfully doing a behavior when certain emotions or intensity of emotion occurs. Examples of daily behaviors that can be practiced in destructive ways are to eat, spend money, use mind or mood altering substances (alcohol, tobacco, caffeine, prescription, or recreational substances), or demonstrate behaviors in an addictive manner (gamble, rage, drink, etc.) or in an unhealthy manner.

These destructive behaviors can accompany "positive" as well as "negative" emotions. Many people over-spend or overindulge in alcohol or food when they are happy and celebrating.

List problematic behaviors and what emotions those behaviors are paired with.

1.

2.

3.

4.

5.

Now list what you can behaviorally do, in each case, to make the emotion have less of a problematic pattern.

1.

2.

3.

4.

5.

Does your partner express that you identify and articulate your feelings clearly? Ask him now and circle the number that best represents his response.

1   2   3   4   5

From your partner's feedback, what small behavior will you do differently around what feeling? State the feeling and the specific behavior.

Are you able to identify and express your emotions in a timely manner? Where are you and where would you like to be?

1   2   3   4   5

Some people are able to identify emotions better in retrospect and are less skilled in the present moment. This would be something to brainstorm, how to effectively process feelings in a timely manner. Strong emotional situations may need a time-out (meaning a let it go for a period of time or for an appropriate setting) or percolating time, both of which would need to be communicated respectfully.

What will you do and/or say when you have emotions occurring in a stressful situation?

How skilled are you at listening to your partner share her feelings? Where would you like to be?

1   2   3   4   5

Specifically, what three things can you do differently to be a better listener with your partner?

1.

2.

3.

It is enough if one tries everyday to comprehend a little of this mystery.

—Albert Einstein

SPIRIT(UAL) HEALTH

These are the basics for doing your spiritual best.

Take time daily for your spirit in a way that nurtures you and is consistent with your values. This can be meditation, song, walking, being in nature, and/or a formal spiritual practice. The important point is to live in a way that is spiritually nurturing for you. This is a crucial piece for balance and wellness. Don't let the brevity of this section belie its importance.

Practicing your spirituality should not be a burden to your health, your partner, or your family. Being a burden to those around you is not spirituality, it is simply self-centeredness and ego practiced under the guise of spirituality.

THOUGHTS OR PSYCHOLOGICAL HEALTH

These are the basics for doing your best with your thoughts (your psychological best).

Learn to check in with yourself. This means bring your awareness to your thoughts on a regular basis many times each day.

- **What is the background noise of your mind?**
- **What is your self-talk saying?**

Many of us live with unchallenged inner critics that make our life harder than it needs to be. Gremlins who endlessly say, "I am stupid." "I am always late." "I am not good enough."

If we (and that is all of us) have these unchallenged tyrants filtering and defining our lives we will not only be miserable, we will probably be contributing to making our partners and our families miserable, too. We will be part of the problem of passing misery on.

Negativity is highly contagious. Thoughts are road signs of what we believe about life such as:

- It is too difficult
- This sucks
- It is easy for others, but hard for me
- I am a victim of life
- It should be fair

- It should be easy
- I cannot be happy because xyz happened to me
- I cannot be happy until xyz happens
- I am not supposed to be here
- This should not be happening to me

Thoughts tend to be self-fulfilling. What are you thinking? Do you notice how it affects what you're doing? Do you notice how it affects the people around you? Do you notice how it affects your sleep, your health, and your energy level?

Fortunately, being positive is even more contagious. Surround yourself with a variety of inspirational people, pictures, books, movies, television, and radio shows. Be wary of people who are very charismatic and have all the answers, even if they have strong and articulate followings. Healthy inspirational people are inclusive, work with diversity and adversity, and are open to discussion, ideas, and growth. People and materials that convey to others through words and deeds the underlying messages of:

- You can do it.
- You can go for it.
- You can make a difference.
- You can keep trying.
- You made a mistake and you can make repairs and learn from it.
- You can still surprise yourself.
- This moment counts. You count.

This is not about Pollyanna thinking; it is about Possibility thinking.

Possibility thinking is not about making your life easy, taking short cuts, or sugarcoating life. It's about motivation and how our brain works best. Your life will tend to flow better if you learn how to use motivation in a healthy way.

Replace energy-draining negative thoughts with motivating thoughts stated in the positive. Do it in writing. Share it with another person.

13 COUPLE CARE

This is a daily needed skill set.

The most important tool for couple care is time. Manage time with calendars, day timers, and planning. To younger or less experienced couples, scheduling your partner in your day timer is, naively, considered unromantic or lacking spontaneity. However, not getting time together is unromantic and eventually damaging. I prefer to think of it as scheduling the rest of the world out. Furthermore, there is plenty of room for spontaneity inside your protected timeframes.

There will be many chapters in your life where couple time will be hard to come by. It is up to you and your partner to protect this precious resource. It is a resource. Finances, a new job, a new baby, teenagers, friends, aging relatives, and illness will present challenges.

COUPLES AND DEVELOPMENTAL AND SITUATIONAL STAGES

As a couple, you need to appreciate and enjoy where you are in your couples journey. Individually and together, participate positively with the "easy" or "up" times as well as the "difficult" times.

It does not help to exaggerate or dramatize whatever stage and context you are experiencing. Float with each part of the journey. Do the best you can. Further, do not demand or expect your friends, family, or colleagues to either be at your stage or even understand your stage or context. Of course, some will be supportive, understanding, and helpful. However, others will be busy at the center of their own experiences. Perhaps you, as a couple, becoming a support to them will help you with your own perspective on your stage of life.

I think of the issue of stage-of-life envy as similar to sibling rivalry. Each child is looking over at the other child to see what she has, does not have, what she is doing and with whom. Frequently, the comparison is used as justification for some "poor me" script your child is developmentally testing.

As a parent, I said to my children when this situation came up (sometimes again and again), "Tell me about you. Who are you? What do you want? What is your situation? What are your goals? How will you achieve your goals? Instead of telling me about your sibling, tell me about you."

Another common problematic focus is to see happiness and fulfillment "over there" or "in the future" or "in the past." Examples of this are:

- Expressing envy for someone with toddlers, lamenting that you're tied down with infants.

- Expressing envy for someone with kids in school because you have toddlers.

- Expressing that you can't wait for xyz stage to come or xyz stage to be over.

- Being happy before we moved here and because we have moved we can't be happy/content/fulfilled here where we are.

- Saying we'll relax when we retire. Until then, we don't have time for relaxation.

- Being romantic when we first met. Now, we are staying busy while we're waiting for that feeling to return.

In each of these examples (and I am sure you can come up with many others), the couple is practicing negative beliefs that tend to be self-fulfilling and are certainly not helpful. In each case, the couple needs to acknowledge where they are in the relationship, what is their developmental stage (together and separately), what is their context (together and separately), and to be actively involved in doing the best they can with the stuff that is currently their life.

This concept is represented in popular phrases, such as:

- Time flies, whether you are having fun or not
- Be here now
- Life is not a dress rehearsal
- This is it

The permutations and possibilities of couples stories are infinite, though there are many common general patterns.

So, be present to participate fully in each stage and context of your life such as:

- Being a single adult
- Building a relationship
- Experiencing loss and grief with family and friends in any stage (this is what I mean about the context of your stage)
- The acquisition stages of knowledge, career, financial stability, health
- The generative stages of children, mentoring, teaching, motivating, encouraging, leading, creating, inventing
- The letting go stages of downsizing, spacious nesting (rather than empty nesting), living simpler
- Being extended family and support personnel to others in the acquisition stages, or challenging financial or health stages
- Being a contributor couple in a supportive role, rather than a central role

Together, you and your partner need to brainstorm how to ergonomically move through these different challenges when they occur.

Bloom where you are.

MANAGING COUPLE TIME

Time management as a couple is the antidote to the "squeaky wheel approach to life" in which you get the leftover time and energy. You get to decide as a couple when and how often to schedule time together, executive time, chore time, relaxation time, social time, and so on. Decide now, with your partner, when is a good time to sit down together, uninterrupted, and make your first meeting to plan your varied couple times for two weeks. Set that forty-five-minute appointment now. Both of you put it on your calendars. You may have to schedule this first meeting two or three weeks in advance.

Here are some recommendations of what you can address at that appointment.

1. Schedule a fun date for just the two of you ***at least once a week*** when possible. What do you enjoy doing together? Set a date and time once a week to practice those things you both enjoy. Examples include:

    *   Movie date
    *   Dinner date
    *   Massage date
    *   Bath date
    *   Coffee shop date
    *   Hiking date
    *   Nature date
    *   Walking date
    *   Biking date
    *   Cooking date
    *   Dancing date
    *   Bowling date
    *   Museum date

You may miss a week due to illness or work. Remember to reset and come back to scheduling a weekly date the next week, or as soon as possible. A date is not about spending money it is about time together and connection.

This is where most couples get off course. They forget to reset to their basic goals and priorities and they get lost, sometimes for years.

2. Schedule a thirty to sixty minute executive session once a week to do things like:

    *   Plan for what is coming up, sync your calendars

    *   Discuss couple business that may include finances, parenting, holiday schedules, chores, communication, car issues and so on

    *   Discuss level of intimacy, both physical and emotional. Plan for intimate time if you are not getting enough of it

    *   Schedule additional executive time if needed

- Schedule individual, couple, and family social calendars

- Use this time to prioritize how you want to spend your time and energy together, separately, and with others

- Review the previous week's or month's calendar for feedback for necessary calendar adjustments. This is critical to address individual and couple balance needs.

  - Did you go over your monthly financial budget?

  - Have you socialized too much or not enough?

  - Are you getting enough exercise?

  - Are you working too much?

  - Are you neglecting your diet or health?

  - Are you neglecting sleep or quiet time?

  - Are you getting too much sleep or quiet time?

  - Are you neglecting your environment? Chores?

  - Are you making love enough?

  - Are you getting enough couple time? Do you need less of one type of couple time and more of another?

  - Are you each getting enough individual time?

  - Are you getting enough family time?

  - Are you getting enough extended-family time?

  - Are you in a rut?

  - Has there been too much change? Too busy? Too stressed?

This is where you evaluate and make purposeful adjustments to how you spend your time individually, as a couple, and as a family.

3. Deliberately schedule a variety of types of couple time weekly and monthly, such as:

- Regular events (shower together, walk together, share a meal together, do chores together, cook together, exercise together).

- Regular intimate events (massage, cuddle, make love, special meal, date).

- Regular social events (dances, classes together, participate in spiritual rituals together).

- Special social events (holidays, birthdays, anniversaries, concerts, theatre, parties).

- Special intimate events (your anniversary, your partner's birthday, acknowledging whatever is important to you and your partner with time, words, and activities).

A BRIEF WORD ABOUT COUPLES BEFORE CHILDREN

Changing from a relationship with two adults to two adults and a baby is a normal couple experience. While each relationship is unique, there is a lot of solid research on the impacts of the different types of parenting and couple relationship patterns on child physical, cognitive, emotional, social, and spiritual development. More of the future is at stake when babies and children are involved. How you communicate and behave as a couple impacts the lifelong script of that nascent individual. Therefore, **working on these skills before children is strongly advised because a very similar skill set can be applied to effective parenting.**

14 FAMILY CARE

CHAPTER

This is a daily needed skill set.

Use the same tools you use for individual and couple care.

- Weekly executive meetings
- Fun family dates
- Calendars and day timers
- Scheduling time
- Balancing time and energy
- Prioritizing time, energy, and resources

Family developmental stage and context is an important piece of information. A new job, a new baby, relocation, stage of development of children, stage of development of aging relatives, and health issues will all impact how you will find balance within the current circumstances.

Your children should be included in planning family care in age appropriate and developmentally appropriate ways as early as possible. This is where you model and teach them about balance. Children who grow up in an environment with exercise, time management, stress management, social connection, and a balanced emphasis on sleep, nutrition, and health tend to repeat that pattern as adults.

Remember, children and adolescent responses are not similar to adult responses. There are normal and predictable developmental differences at different ages. If you're not knowledgeable about child development information, you're making your life unnecessarily difficult and shortchanging your child. The developmental stages of infants, toddlers, children, preadolescents, middle adolescents, and late adolescents present some of the most interesting challenges and stimulations of being a parent.

COUPLES WITH YOUNG CHILDREN DESERVE EXTRA EMPHASIS AND SUPPORT

If you're a couple with young children, chances are there are not enough hours in the day or days in the week. You will need, and you deserve, support in a variety of areas. If there are healthy adults who can help you with their participation in time and/or energy, please find a balanced way to use that help. Connect with other young families and share ideas, and be resources for each other. It's overwhelming and isolating to be a young family without a support network.

Keep in mind the "bloom where you are" concept. Learn to arrange your life in a developmentally appropriate and realistic child-centered way. For example, with infants in the first year of life you may want to:

- Have lots of early to bed nights because you will have many early mornings
- Accept a different level of disarray and organization in your home
- Accept that you both may be tired more often
- Accept that you will not be as socially spontaneous as in the past
- Accept that you will go out less and travel less

This is all developmentally normal. It will be important in your weekly couples meeting to address the naturally occurring challenges and imbalances, and carefully plan for smaller periods of couple care and self-care.

At the beginning of parenthood, it's often overwhelming to take a shower and get dressed. However, in a very short time you're amazed at how much you can accomplish with a baby attached to your body.

Thoughtfully and deliberately, add in couple and self-care activities and routines, such as exercise time, dinner out, and finding a relaxing time to make love. These are important activities to work back into your calendar again and again.

The trap to avoid is living parallel lives at this busy, wonderful, and overwhelming time; lives where one partner specializes in kids and the other in the rest of the world, and you infrequently connect and overlap.

Infants, toddlers, kids, preteens, and teens all need the active nurturing involvement of both parents throughout their lives. They also need the daily modeling of communication, respect, love, honor, disagreement, joy and fun, to name a few. They benefit from the modeling of a loving couples relationship.

Concrete recommendations for couples with young kids:

- Schedule an executive session once a week.

- Schedule a date once a week.

- Schedule regular exercise.

- Schedule bill paying time together.

- Schedule housecleaning time together.

- Attend to Self-care and Couple Care.

- Take a parenting workshop or class.

- Take a child development workshop or class.

- Have friends in similar circumstances.

- Have mentors who have been through similar circumstances.

- Have a list of resources: names of sitters, standing dates for sitters, helpful extended family members, neighbors, friends who could help in a pinch or who are just good family companions.

- Try to set things up on a repeating weekly or monthly schedule, such as executive session on Saturday mornings from 9:00 to 10:00, date night Thursday from 5:00 to 8:30 with a standing babysitter, all doctor appointments and other health appointments on Tuesday afternoons. This way, you do not find yourself trying to reinvent a schedule every week.

- Be flexible where you can, and be structured where you need to be.

You will have other times in your life where you won't need the same level of structure. This stage will pass. The people who are fully participatory and present for this part of their lives are enriched by the experience. They have continuing pleasure, love, and connection out of every moment. Parents, who cut corners, are destructively selfish and self-centered, even when it comes to their children, are the ones who live with regrets.

15 TAKE TIME TO PLAY, ENJOY, AND HAVE FUN

CHAPTER

This is a daily and weekly needed skill set.

Joy and play are a very important part of physical health, mental health, and relational health. Joy and play affect communication, intimacy, sexuality, spirituality, and parenting.

The dictionary definition of *play* is "to engage in an activity for enjoyment rather than a serious or practical purpose." My definition of *play* is "to engage in a healthy activity for enjoyment." Healthy play for the sake of enjoyment is a necessary and practical purpose in and of itself.

Trauma research has shown that play is one of the better therapeutic ways for children to process through grief, loss, and trauma.

Play is <u>never</u> at the expense of another. Therefore, teasing, unwanted tickling, sarcasm, and coercion are <u>not</u> play activities, even if these activities were "play" in your family of origin. Teasing, unwanted tickling, sarcasm, and coercion are displays of power; they are not shared fun.

Play is enjoyable for everyone involved. In a relationship, one partner and the relationship should not suffer imbalances because of the other partner's individual play activities. Conversely, one partner's seriousness and lack of play should not control the relationship.

Because life can be hard, we tend to justify and solidify that difficulty with unnecessary drama and seriousness. Sadly, for some, life becomes too important to play and have fun.

It's healthy, life affirming, and therapeutic to experience joy, lightness, and laughter. It's physically and relationally beneficial to have your problems and seriousness drop away because you are focused on the joyful experience of the moment.

It's important to find little ways to experience playful moments throughout your day. Use cartoons, jokes, interactive games (that involve people and laughter), music, and dance to accomplish this.

The benefits of play carry over to the rest of your life. Play nurtures your body and your brain. It supports creativity, connection and balance.

Can you let go of your inappropriate seriousness for the sake of living fully?

You and your partner each make a list of ten things you consider playful. Make a date and share your lists with each other. Some activities you will do alone or with other people and some you will do together as a couple with or without other people. Some activities will be very simple, such as I like to read *Far Side* cartoons in the morning. Money should not be necessary for healthy playfulness. Make these lists part of your relationship guide. Update them as needed.

This is another area where couples can start getting off track. There are seemingly unimportant things you like to do or enjoy which you don't think are important enough to speak up about. One or both partners may too often withhold an opinion for the sake of going along, ease, or expedience. As an occasional event, this is not a relationship problem. As a regular unexamined pattern, it creates relationship imbalance and too often results in negative thoughts, emotions, and behaviors.

Communicating with your partner about your needs, wants, and preferences even in everyday situations or seemingly unimportant situations builds connection. Communicating what you want and getting what you want are two different things. There is still the work of negotiation and compromise. However, you also get to learn more about each other.

This is glue for the relationship. Neglecting to share who you are, what you feel, and what you prefer leads to negative self-talk and resentment.

ENJOYMENT AND FUN (Partner A)

List some playful activities. After each activity put I = individually or C = as a couple for the activity. Some may have both. Ideally, you have about five of each.

What partner A considers playful:

1.
2.
3.
4.
5.
6.
7.
8.
9.
10.

What partner B considers playful:

1.
2.
3.
4.
5.
6.
7.
8.
9.
10.

All the world is birthday cake,
so take a piece but not too much.

—George Harrison

WORKSHEET

ENJOYMENT AND FUN (Partner B)

List some playful activities. After each activity put I = individually or C = as a couple for the activity. Some may have both. Ideally, you have about five of each.

What partner A considers playful:

1.

2.

3.

4.

5.

6.

7.

8.

9.

10.

What partner B considers playful:

1.

2.

3.

4.

5.

6.

7.

8.

9.

10.

All the world is birthday cake,
so take a piece but not too much.

—George Harrison

TAKE TIME FOR INTIMACY

This is a daily and weekly needed skill set.

In general, women tend to want and need emotional intimacy as a foundation for physical intimacy and men tend to want and need physical intimacy as a foundation for emotional intimacy.

"In general" means it is a common gender dynamic. It may or may not be the case for you and your partner. Different intimacy needs is an issue in same-sex relationships so it is not just about gender.

Decide with your partner whether emotional intimacy or physical intimacy is easier to discuss and then work on that topic first. If you disagree on which to work on first, toss a coin for an odd-even schedule. This means during the odd weeks of the month (the first and third weeks), one dimension takes priority, and during the even weeks (second and fourth), the other dimension is the priority. If you have part of a month remaining, you can do both or take a break for those few days.

EMOTIONAL INTIMACY

Nurturing Each Other Emotionally Does a Body and a Relationship Good.

The Five to One Ratio

Gottman's research found that happily married couples have a minimum ratio of 5:1 good interactions to bad.

It's not the number of bad interactions that determines couples' relationships ending. Rather, it's the number of bad interactions relative to the number of good interactions.

If couples have few good interactions, if there is a lack of nurturing, then when bad times happen there's *not enough glue* (resilience) built into the relationship to withstand the difficulties for very long. However, if a couple battles quite a bit and they also do plenty of nurturing and loving (more than five times relative to the battling) then their relationship likely will survive. Relationships with ratio's greater than 5:1 tend to thrive.

Definition of nurture: To care for and encourage, to cherish

Make a list of what each of you considers nurturing behavior. The reason this is important is the receiver of the nurturing gets to decide what is nurturing for her. You do not get to decide for the other person. Chances are, while there may be a lot of overlap (you both like long walks on the beach at sunset), there usually are significant differences. Here is a list of some ideas and examples for this exercise.

State your general "nurturing" concept clearly and succinctly and give ten examples. Do not skimp on this exercise; give a minimum of ten examples. The examples should be stated in the positive, i.e. what you want, *not* what you don't want. For example, the negative statement "Don't wake me on Saturday morning" stated in the positive is "I want to sleep in on Saturday morning." Stated more specifically and in the positive is, "I want to sleep in on Saturday morning until 9:30 a.m." A person more used to nurturing others than receiving nurturing may struggle to get ten examples. It is worth the effort.

Examples of This Exercise

Nurturing Concept: Express appreciation for me both verbally and physically on a daily basis.

These are specific examples of what expressing appreciation verbally sounds like for me.

1. Use the words *please* and *thank you*.
2. "I thought of how much I love you today when I was ... and I just wanted to let you know."
3. Say "I love you" on a daily basis.
4. I look forward to us being alone together tonight for dinner.
5. I know (my cousins, parents, boss) can be draining for you. Thank you for giving up an evening to be with them.
6. Coming home to you is a wonderful part of my day.
7. You handled that (trying, difficult, tedious) situation well.
8. Can I help?
9. You make me laugh.
10. How about a date out next Thursday evening? Do you have a particular place you would like? If not, how about your favorite Indian or Italian restaurant? I'll get a sitter.

These are specific examples of what expressing appreciation nonverbally looks like to me.

1. Initiate a long (thirty second) hug when we have been apart for more than four or five hours.
2. Hold hands in public.
3. Hold each other as we watch television.
4. Give me a foot rub.
5. Give me a back rub.
6. Initiate housework without being asked, reminded, or prompted.
7. Let me finish my thoughts without interruption.
8. Make eye contact with me when you are expressing affection.
9. Make the bed together.
10. Take my hand as we cross the street.

Nurturing Concept: Do fun activities together.

These are specific examples of my idea of doing fun things together. I would like us to plan on Sunday evening to do one of these activities together weekly.

1. Go to a funny movie together at the discount movie theatre.
2. Go for an hour walk together with the dogs around sunset.
3. Go on an hour bike ride together.
4. Go to a concert or game together.
5. Have a barbeque dinner outside with the neighbors.
6. Play scrabble once a week in the evening.
7. Bake bread together.
8. Go to a lecture together.
9. Have a picnic lunch at the park on the weekend.
10. Go to the theatre for a live show.

Nurturing Concept: Be more social as a couple.

I would like us to do something social as a couple with others twice a month. We can plan the last week of each month for the next month. Once we decide on the people, the date, and the activity, I will work on solidifying the arrangements by the first of the month on even months and you can do the nailing down of plans on the odd months.

1. Have another couple over for dinner.
2. Go to someone else's house for dinner.
3. Go dancing with friends.
4. Have friends over for fun and games (board games, card games, interactive games).
5. Go to a community potluck or fundraiser together.
6. Go camping with friends or family.
7. Go out to dinner with friends you have not seen in a while.
8. Volunteer at the food bank together on Sundays for the month of February
9. Take a class together. Conversational Spanish, Swing, Current Events, Couples Enrichment.
10. Join a book group together

Nurturing Concept: Give me a break, a rest (from the busyness).

Now that (tax season is over, high season is over, the kids are home for the summer, your parents are visiting, the holidays are here, etc.) I'd like some additional personal time. I'm flexible. Here are some of my ideas. Let's decide what will work for both of us.

1. Sleep in one morning a week. We can decide together what morning is most doable.
2. Have a no TV day twice a week, preferably one evening a week and one weekend day
3. Go to bed earlier once a week
4. Arrange for someone else to do the shopping for two weeks.
5. Take a yoga class Thursday evenings for six weeks.
6. Arrange for someone else to pick the kids up on Fridays this month.

7. Let the voice mail answer the phone after 6:00 p.m.

8. Have a morning in bed together one Sunday a month.

9. Have a half hour of reading time after dinner three evenings a week.

10. Have a weekend in the house alone without responsibilities some time in the next two months. Say from Saturday noon until Sunday at 4:00 p.m. You, the kids, and the dogs can visit your grandparents.

Nurturing Concept: Add something new. Surprise me.

I feel we're in a rut. Let's give each other a list of potential spice and surprises and here is mine. Maybe we can do something new and spicy two or three times a week for each other.

1. Put on some music and dance with me on the weekend.

2. Hide my favorite chocolate in an unlikely place for discovery.

3. Surprise me with scented massage oil (Remembering I like mild and fruity scents).

4. Make a romantic dinner setting (candles, lighting, music).

5. Go somewhere we used to go to and loved, but have not done for a long time, an old restaurant, park, or a walk in our old neighborhood.

6. Have an evening of "pretend no electricity" from 4:00 p.m. until bedtime.

7. Plan a weekend getaway to somewhere we have never been before with a limited budget.

8. Make love other than in our bed half the time.

9. Surprise me with a single rose or a small personal gift (not expensive) at work.

10. Design a romantic card for me.

11. Work out together on the weekend and have a long shower together.

After you have your written concept and ten positively stated examples, make a date to share them with your partner. Neatness and creativity count. You should each have your own copy to keep.

It's not your partner's job to check off all ten items as fast as possible and throw away the list. It's her role as a nurturer to be aware of your wants and practice the nurturing activities where possible as frequently as possible. Neither is your partner mandated to do all the activities on your list. If six out of ten of the ideas work for both of you, then start there. There are still elements of negotiation in this process. These are your personal guides for taking good care of each other. Treasure them and use them to strengthen the bonds in your relationship.

There are four copies of the Emotional Intimacy, Nurturing worksheet. Each create one for your partner and one for yourself or your relationship guide.

EMOTIONAL INTIMACY, NURTURING (Partner A)

NURTURING CONCEPT:

TEN SPECIFIC EXAMPLES:

1.

2.

3.

4.

5.

6.

7.

8.

9.

10.

Those who give with joy,
that joy is their reward.

—Kahlil Gibran

EMOTIONAL INTIMACY, NURTURING (Partner A for Partner B)

NURTURING CONCEPT:

TEN SPECIFIC EXAMPLES:

1.

2.

3.

4.

5.

6.

7.

8.

9.

10.

Those who give with joy,
that joy is their reward.

—Kahlil Gibran

EMOTIONAL INTIMACY, NURTURING (Partner B)

NURTURING CONCEPT:

TEN SPECIFIC EXAMPLES:

1.

2.

3.

4.

5.

6.

7.

8.

9.

10.

Those who give with joy,
that joy is their reward.

—Kahlil Gibran

EMOTIONAL INTIMACY, NURTURING (Partner B for Partner A)

NURTURING CONCEPT:

TEN SPECIFIC EXAMPLES:

1.

2.

3.

4.

5.

6.

7.

8.

9.

10.

Those who give with joy,
that joy is their reward.

—Kahlil Gibran

PHYSICAL INTIMACY

Touch And Sex Do A Body And A Relationship Good

Research shows that regular emotionally connected sexual expression is beneficial to one's health.

The parts of you that benefit include your heart, blood pressure, circulation, immune system, and brain, to name a few. Intimate and fun sex creates endorphins and a sense of well-being. It improves mood. It improves communication. It adds to quality of life and to the lifespan.

If it is so beneficial and it feels so good,

Why do so many couples
Make enjoying their sexuality
Such a low priority in their lives?

My short answer is: Too busy, too tired, rigid roles, power struggles, poor body image, poor self-esteem, neglect, fear, resentment, and anger.

Hint: The other chapters in this book are as important to fulfilling healthy sexuality as this chapter is.

I believe impaired couples' sexuality is a community health care issue that negatively affects health, relationships, families, parenting, and communities.

Couples need to be encouraged to learn about and practice healthy sexuality.

This physically intimate part of a relationship exists within the context and subtext of the whole relationship. If communication is poor, if respect and collaboration are low, if you're out of balance individually, as a couple, or as a family and have been for a long time, it will affect sexual intimacy and sexual satisfaction. Conversely, if sexual intimacy is not occurring or sexual satisfaction is low for one or both partners, then that dynamic will negatively effect couple communication, respect, and collaboration.

For most people talking about one's sexuality can be especially vulnerable. We do not want our feelings hurt and we do not want to hurt our partner's feelings.

It is important to remember that sex with your partner is a physical give and take. It is dynamic. Change, negotiation, differing views, and preferences are the norm.

Overcoming emotional discomfort regarding sexuality and sensuality is a critical couple's growing experience.

The goal is actually a process. The goal is to have a sexual conversation that can evolve in the moment and over time.

This is the best part:

It can evolve verbally, physically, emotionally,
and spiritually over time, or in a heartbeat.

Where you are now in your relationship does not limit where you can go, and the many expressions of your coupleness are

As unique and diverse as each of you are individually.

If you make *sensuality, creativity, spirituality, and fun* a priority in your life, the wealth of healthy sexuality is priceless. This is not necessarily about "getting more," it's about "getting a better connection on every level." (Although, when you get a better connection there usually tends to be more.)

We have all experienced some situational conditions that are temporarily sexually disabling or diminishing. Not feeling well, medication side effects, a new baby, having a toddler, having a teenager, work–work–work, accident, trauma, or grief can individually and together pile up in life and push out sensuality and sexuality.

When this happens, and it will, it is critical to take the time to reset and bring mutually satisfying sensuality and sexuality back into your life.

Are you willing to work for it?

Are you willing to give your partner what he wants and needs most in the relationship such as acknowledgment, respect, appreciation, touch, and time?

Are you willing to experience the excitement of emotional risk with each other on a physical and spiritual level?

The choice is yours as a couple

To pursue this option

Both together,

One alone

Or

Not at all

It takes two to say yes and only one to say no. However, the yes person can still grow and has many healthy options. I recommend finding a book that suits you in the Health and Sexuality section of your local book store. Take an hour to browse through the books in the section, or find a used copy online. There are many, many good ones from which to choose.

Here are some common couple patterns that negatively impact sexual desire:

1. You take turns being angry or resentful

2. One of you specializes in being angry or resentful and the other caters to it

3. You don't work through the usual problematic emotional or behavioral baggage

4. Sex is unsatisfactory in some way and you're afraid to hurt your partner's feelings by discussing it

5. You take your partner for granted

6. You are out of balance physically, psychologically, or emotionally in a significant way for an extended period

If you avoid addressing negative patterns, you are sometimes individually, and oftentimes together, making choices that support an impoverished sexual relationship with yourself and your partner.

If you want a closer connection with your partner, say that to him **now** *and then read on.*

Each partner completes Worksheet 16.2 individually. This alone may be a stretch for some people and it is OK to stretch and grow through the process.

Make a date to share some of your thoughts, feelings, and preferences with your partner. Set the stage with a demonstration of what a romantic environment is for you as practice and as an example. Share only what you are ready to, leaning a little on the stretching side.

One partner at a time becomes the question poser while the other partner uses his worksheet to help him answer the questions in a conversational manner. Sometimes we forget what we want to share when discussing emotionally vulnerable information. Your completed worksheet is there to help as a guide.

The question poser's role is now to be a *safe and attentive listener*.

After you have completed the one-way sharing, thank your partner for being a safe listener, give him nonverbal and verbal appreciation and reverse roles.

If time is a consideration and you cannot give the exercise your full attention, break it into manageable parts where you can. Fifteen to thirty minutes for each segment (filling out questionnaire separately, one sharing, other sharing) may be a realistic guideline.

Notice that discussion and brainstorming are not part of this initial sharing. It's about listening to who your partner is and what are his likes, dislikes, preferences, fantasies, and desires.

It is important to remember:

- This is not a one-time conversation; it is one conversation in an ongoing process
- It is okay to share your preferences, and sharing your preferences does not mean the other person has to accommodate everything you choose to share
- It is okay to stretch in your requests
- It is okay to stretch in your willingness to please yourself
- It is okay to stretch in your willingness to please your partner
- It is okay to say no respectfully

Be gentle and supportive with your partner as he shares.

EXAMPLES FOR WORKSHEETS 16.2 AND 16.3:

Sexual overtures that I like:

- "Would you like to have a romantic rendezvous Saturday, late morning?" This is accompanied by eye contact and caressing of my hand or arm.
- "I want to make love to you." Accompany this statement by cuddling and snuggling on the couch, in the car, or on the way home.
- "How about a romantic shower?"

Sexual overtures that turn me off:

- Lack of an overture
- Grabbing my breasts while I am in the kitchen
- Grabbing my butt
- Rolling over in the morning with morning breath and expecting sex without any foreplay
- Not being freshly showered or clean
- Waking me up abruptly in the middle of the night for sex

These are foreplay activities I like:

- A ten-minute foot massage
- A ten-minute feather touch back massage
- Long slow kisses and slow caressing all over
- Digital sex for later foreplay
- Oral sex for later foreplay

These are foreplay activities that turn me off:

- Being unwashed
- Bad breath
- Digital sex or oral sex before I am ready
- The television being on
- Being in a rush
- Not using quality lubrication
- Being distracted

I would prefer to enjoy foreplay for a minimum and maximum of:

- Five minutes when we are short on time but want to have a quickie
- Ten minutes is better than five but still on the short side
- Fifteen minutes is more like it
- Thirty minutes is a luxury

Things we do that turn me on:

- Play sensuous music
- Light candles
- Share massages with scented oil
- Clean sheets
- New places to have sex
- Occasionally trying new sexual positions
- Use fantasy and erotic conversation
- Take a bath or shower together before we make love

Things I would like to try:

- Using a sex toy such as tingly gel or cream
- Using a vibrator
- Oral sex
- One partner at a time bringing the other to a slow erotic orgasm
- Making love outside on our deck on a no moon night

Things I would like us to do to grow sexually:

- Go to the bookstore together and buy two books about sexuality and sexual expression
- Have a special date to talk about what we enjoy and would like to try every other month
- Get away for a night or a weekend every season

My ideal frequency for having sex is _____ times a month.

My minimum frequency for having sex is _____ times a month.

Keep in mind these frequencies change depending on circumstances such as, a new job, having the flu, pregnancy, being under a deadline, dealing with life complications such as houseguests, lack of sleep, disrupted sleep, and health issues.

After each of you has done the uninterrupted sharing exercise, you can schedule sexual brainstorming and problem-solving conversations as desired. You may need to do some reading for ideas. A one-hour date to browse books on sexuality at the library or bookstore may be a nice couples date. Nurture your couples sexuality with feedback and open hearts. Use the Brainstorming and Problem-Solving Guides in Chapter 9 for addressing sexuality and sensuality.

Having a sexual check-in meeting a minimum of every other month may be adequate, if both of you are finding your sexual and sensual expression creative and nurturing.

If you are working at enjoyment, relaxation, excitement, reciprocity, or expanding your sexual awareness, expression, or boundaries in some way, you may want to have sexual feedback meetings more frequently.

Health Note: The extremes of the bell curve in sexual frequency need qualified professional consultation. Over 20 percent of married couples are not having sex. The research definition of not having sex, as a couple, is a frequency of less than ten times a year (when there are no extenuating circumstances). If, by this definition, you have not had sex for a while, I recommended you attend to this as a health issue, a mental health issue, and a relational issue. You may need professional consultation.

The other extreme, having sex every day and often multiple times of day, is an emotional, psychological, and relational red flag. If the demand for sex is regularly that high in frequency, then chances are, other emotions and issues are not being addressed adequately in the relationship. This is not sensual intimate sex as much as it is a health issue or an anxious addiction. Addictive sex is a mental health issue that typically drains a couple's relationship.

Further, if either extreme is an issue and it has been more than a year since either of you have had a medical wellness check, you may want to schedule an appointment and rule out medical and medication issues. Many health issues and medications have sexual side effects.

You do the best this day, then see what the next day brings. You never know how much you grow in a day.

—from the movie *Hope Floats*

PHYSICAL INTIMACY (Partner A)

These are sexual overtures that I like:

These are sexual overtures that turn me off:

These are foreplay activities I like:

These are foreplay activities that turn me off:

I would prefer to enjoy foreplay for a minimum of:

And a maximum of:

These are things we do that turn me on:

These are things I would like to try:

These are things I am not willing to try at this time:

Frequency of physical intimacy:
My ideal MMR (Minimum Monthly Requirement) for making love is:
My minimal MMR is:

Young lovers seek perfection,
old lovers learn the art of sew-
ing shreds together and of seeing
beauty in a multiplicity of patches.

—from the movie
How To Make An American Quilt

PHYSICAL INTIMACY (Partner B)

These are sexual overtures that I like:

These are sexual overtures that turn me off:

These are foreplay activities I like:

These are foreplay activities that turn me off:

I would prefer to enjoy foreplay for a minimum of:

And a maximum of:

These are things we do that turn me on:

These are things I would like to try:

These are things I am not willing to try at this time:

Frequency of physical intimacy:
My ideal MMR (Minimum Monthly Requirement) for making love is:
My minimal MMR is:

Young lovers seek perfection,
old lovers learn the art of sew-
ing shreds together and of seeing
beauty in a multiplicity of patches.

—from the movie
How To Make An American Quilt

OUR PHYSICAL INTIMACY

These are sexual overtures that we will try:

These are foreplay activities we will try:

We would prefer to enjoy foreplay for a minimum of:

And a maximum of:

These are things we do that turn one or both of us on:

These are things we would like to try together:

Average frequency of physical intimacy:

Partner A's MMR is 12 times a month, Partner B's is 3 times a month.

12 + 3 = 15 and 15 divided by 2 = 7.5, rounded to 7 or 8.

This frequency may be practiced in a number of ways. Two times a week for a month or three times a week alternating with one time a week for a month. Then discuss how it worked for each of you. Keep what worked and try something different for the next month.

Our target MMR ideal for this next month is:

Our minimum MMR for the month is ____. (Below this level and you start bickering over otherwise uneventful issues, something I call "verbal sex" because the bickering seems to diminish if the couple achieves the experiential communication of making love).

You make the past mean different things by how you use the time that comes after.

—Captain Fancy on *NYPD Blue*

17 TAKE TIME FOR FINANCES

This is a daily, weekly, monthly, quarterly, and annually needed skill set.

Like sexuality, if finance is a taboo subject or is not functioning well it will negatively affect every aspect of your relationship and your life. If you can read this chapter aloud to each other, and discuss finance's impact and meaning in your relationship openly, then you have an indicator that finance is not a taboo subject in your relationship.

In American culture, the dimension of finance is too often out of balance. Overemphasizing the financial dimension can take as much of a relational toll as an unstable financial situation.

When finances are overemphasized, relationships tend to be emotionally and psychologically immature. Generally, they play out a drama of fragile egos because the external measure of "how much you have or don't have" distracts energy from other important relationship dimensions such as communication, emotions, and sensuality. *Financial balance supports a healthy relationship.*

When finances are unstable, relationships tend to be preoccupied with basic living issues such as housing, food, healthcare, and information technology. *Financial stability supports a healthy relationship.*

Since housework and childcare are a significant cost for most couples, in either time or money, they are included in this financial chapter. Your financial situation affects how you address these ongoing daily needs.

There continue to be gender differences in how financial pressures are experienced even in the twenty-first century. Both men and women feel significant financial pressure to succeed. However, women's self-esteem as it relates to financial health is mediated by other dimensions that are also very important to women's identities, such as family relationships, friendship, and spirituality. Additionally, women, unlike men, can legitimately earn social credit marrying a financially successful male.

Men, on the other hand, are judged foremost on the dimension of finance. All their self-esteem eggs are too often in one basket. Men may be out of shape, and socially obnoxious, but if they make "a lot of money," they're considered successful. A man may be emotionally unsupportive of his wife and children, but if he makes "a lot of money," he's considered successful in most social circles.

Conversely, if a man is not producing "enough" in the financial dimension, he's often considered less successful. If he is the stay-at-home parent, he's frequently judged as less productive. Society has a double standard valuing parenting time, housework, and outside work when it comes to gender.

If you are a couple where there is significant financial inequity in either resources or knowledge about financial resources, check if there are self-esteem, or power and control issues. It doesn't help a couple to ignore the financial lens and how it affects the fit in your relationship.

Talking about financial inequities in the relationship with respect and under-standing can add to your sense of connection with each other. As a couple, dis-cuss your current financial state and your financial skill levels. If it's not pos-sible to discuss finances as a couple without strife, consult with a marriage and family therapist, a financial planner, or a respected and skilled third party.

1. What are your feelings about gender and income? Is one of you more "in charge" of financial decisions, income or cash flow? How was that decision made? How is the current arrangement working for each of you?

2. What are your feelings about gender and roles such as house-work and childcare?

3. How do you share housework if you are both working full time outside the home? How do you share housework if you have a significant income difference? How do you share housework if one of you works at home or is a stay-at-home parent?

4. How do finances affect your decision making as a couple? Does the person with less income have less say? How do fi-nances affect power issues in your relationship?

These issues come up again and again in couples' relationships as the context of the relationship changes. Relocation, unemployment, returning to school, pregnancy, parenting, retiring, and health issues are some of the more com-mon financial and role change challenges.

It is in a couple's best interest for both members to have basic financial man-agement knowledge and set realistic financial goals together. Understanding and being able to communicate about cash flow, saving, investment, credit, debt, and budgets are crucial to a healthy relationship. We all need these basic financial literacy skills.

Basic financial skills include:

1. Communicating about finances in a variety of circumstances (see Communication, Chapters 6 through 10)
2. Understanding how much money is coming in and how much money is going out
3. Accounting for and tracking the financial flow
4. Planning a realistic budget
5. Planning for future financial stability
6. Living within a budget

If you don't know how to account for the financial inflow and outflow you have, even if it is a negative cash flow every month, how will you know how to manage financial abundance? If you have financial abundance, and are not managing it well, chances are that, at a minimum, you will be wasteful or you may inadvertently create your own difficult financial circumstances in the future.

Have a conversation with your partner about what money means to each of you. Use these questions as a starting place for a series of fifteen minute discussions on your financial skills, wellness, and goals.

- What would you like your relationship with money to be?
- What feelings do you associate with money? Self-importance? Security? Safety? Entitlement? Stability? Shame? Fear? Fun? Entertainment? Success?
- What did money mean to you growing up? How did your parents manage their finances? Were there gender issues related to money?
- How would you rate your money management skills? What financial skills do you want to develop? What financial values do you want to practice?
- Do you both contribute ideas to the couple's financial vision?
- Is money a secret? Is spending a secret? Is debt a secret? Is accounting for how money is spent a problem?
- Do you have similar financial goals around saving, debt, investment, and risk? Where do you differ? How do you talk about that difference?

- Do you have biases around gender and income? Does one partner "have to" earn more than the other? If earning capacity switched, how would it affect your relationship?

- If you own property, do you own it jointly? Are assets in both names? If one of you died suddenly, would the surviving partner have the knowledge and skill to manage financially?

Add your own questions to the outline and discussion topics.

Sometimes one or both partners use ignorance and denial of financial responsibility as an excuse for poor money management. That decision only hurts and stresses the relationship. *The ergonomically fit couple makes it a goal to have regular financial status meetings.*

Schedule a financial meeting with your partner *now*. Agree upon a time and put it in your calendars.

The following are four worksheets to fill out and update on a regular basis. If you have trouble filling out a monthly cash flow statement, you may need to keep very detailed records of every dollar earned and spent on a daily basis for three to six months, summarizing each month to get an accurate picture of what is happening financially.

MONTHLY CASH FLOW

MONTHLY INCOME (after taxes)

Income/salary from all sources
Other income   Total Monthly Income _____

MONTHLY EXPENSES

Housing

Mortgage/Rent
Association Dues
Yard Care
Housing Maintenance
Housing Repair

Total Housing _____

Utilities

Gas
Electricity
Water
Garbage
Phone
Cell phone
Internet access
Cable
Other

Total Utilities _____

Insurance

Homeowners/Renters
Health
Medical
Life
Disability
Other

Total Insurance _____

Personal Care

Educational
Child Care
Health Related (e.g. Massage)
Pharmacy
Health Club
Other (Hair, nails)

Total Personal Care _____

Clothing

New clothes & shoes
Dry cleaning
Other

Total Clothes _____

Food

Groceries
Eating out
Other (Alcohol, Pet Food)

Total Food _____

Transportation

Public transit
Car loan/lease
Car insurance
Maintenance
Parking
Gas
Other

Total Transportation _____

Loans/Lines of Credit

Credit Card
Home Equity Loan/Line
Personal Loan/Line
Education Loans
Other

Total Loans _____

Entertainment & Recreation

Movies
Vacation
Parties
Other

Total Entertainment _____

Miscellaneous

Gifts
Books
Office Supplies
Subscriptions
Other

Total Miscellaneous _____

Total Monthly Expenses _____

TOTAL MONTHLY INCOME – TOTAL MONTHLY EXPENSES = NET CASH FLOW _____

ASSETS AND LIABILITIES

Date:

Update quarterly or semiannually

List Assets: (house, car, savings, stock)

List Liabilities: (mortgage or rent, loans, credit card debt, medical debt, unpaid bills and taxes, child support)

What is your credit rating?

What do you want it to be?

What are your goals in the next year for these assets and liabilities?

ANNUAL FINANCIAL HEALTH PLAN

Date:

Review monthly. Update as needed.

Plan to pay off debt:

Monthly:

Annually:

Plan to increase income:

Monthly:

Annually:

Plan to decrease outflow:

Daily:

Weekly:

Monthly:

Annually:

Plan to increase savings:

Monthly:

Annually:

Only that day dawns to which we are awake.

—Henry David Thoreau

TAKING STOCK OF YOUR FINANCIAL STRENGTHS AND CHALLENGES

List your financial strengths.

	PARTNER A	PARTNER B
1.		
2.		
3.		
4.		

List your financial challenges.

	PARTNER A	PARTNER B
1.		
2.		
3.		

List skills you would like to learn or better develop.

	PARTNER A	**PARTNER B**
1.		
2.		
3.		
4.		
5.		

Prioritize the list and write a specific plan for how each of you will acquire the skills and by what date.

At a minimum

- Have a monthly financial planning session updating income, outflow, and priorities; and
- Have a monthly (or you pick the frequency) work session. The work sessions are for paying bills, balancing checkbooks, auditing bills, following up on financial reports, updates, or record keeping.

Put the meeting dates for both planning and work sessions on the calendar now.

18 YOUR RELATIONSHIP TOOLBOX

CHAPTER

This is a daily needed skill set.

These are some tools for your relationship toolbox. Just like a toolbox in the garage or the closet, keep these tools in a safe and accessible place. Keep them updated and in good repair, and add new tools as you discover them. Similar to any other toolbox, you don't use a tool once and discard it. They're too valuable. The combination of your personal relationship guide, your toolbox, and your willingness to use them are your gift to each other.

Go over the list every few months to remind yourself what relationship tools are at your fingertips. Practice and successful repetition of use is the key.

Time

Day timers, calendars

Personal Relationship Guide (periodically updated)

Executive session dates

Realistic behavioral goals

Operational Behavioral Plans

Follow through

Feedback

Identify challenges

Brainstorm

Problem solve

Play dates

Healthy social support network

Awareness of thoughts

Awareness of feelings

Awareness of behaviors

Tolerate your discomfort for growth

Tolerate your partner's discomfort for growth

Accept and work with your mistakes

Accept and work with your partner's mistakes

Not take things personally, Q-TIP (Quit Taking It Personally)

Let go

Forgive

Nurture yourself

Nurture your partner

Accept nurturing from your partner

Accept delayed gratification

Put plans in writing

Review plans daily, weekly, or monthly

Revise plans in writing as needed

Celebrate small accomplishments

19 CELEBRATE YOUR RELATIONSHIP

CHAPTER

This is a skill set to do today.

Appreciate Yourself,
Your Partner,
and
Your Relationship
Everyday.

How can you do it right now?

It's up to you. Yeah! You!

—John Lennon,
Instant Karma

A FEELINGS

FEELINGS INVENTORY

This inventory is from Marshall Rosenberg's book *Non-Violent Communication: A Language of Life (2003) and is reproduced with permission.*

The following are words we use when we want to express a combination of emotional states and physical sensations.

This list is neither exhaustive nor definitive. It's a starting place to support anyone who wishes to engage in a process of deepening self-discovery and to facilitate greater understanding and connection between people.

There are two parts to this list:

1. **Feelings we may have when our needs are being met**
2. **Feelings we may have when our needs are not being met**

AFFECTIONATE
Compassionate
Friendly
Loving
Open Hearted
Sympathetic
Tender
Warm

CONFIDENT
Empowered
Open
Proud
Safe
Secure

ENGAGED
Absorbed
Alert
Curious
Engrossed
Enchanted
Entranced
Fascinated
Interested
Intrigued
Involved
Spellbound
Stimulated

INSPIRED
Amazed
Awed
Wonder

EXCITED
Amazed
Animated
Ardent
Aroused
Astonished
Dazzled
Eager
Energetic
Enthusiastic
Giddy
Invigorated
Lively
Passionate
Surprised
Vibrant

EXHILARATED
Blissful
Ecstatic
Elated
Enthralled

Exuberant
Radiant
Rapturous
Thrilled

GRATEFUL
Appreciative
Moved
Thankful
Touched

HOPEFUL
Expectant
Encouraged
Optimistic

JOYFUL
Amused
Delighted
Glad
Happy
Jubilant
Pleased
Tickled

PEACEFUL
Calm
Clear Headed
Comfortable
Centered
Content
Equanimous
Fulfilled
Mellow
Quiet
Relaxed
Relieved
Satisfied
Serene
Still
Tranquil
Trusting

REFRESHED
Enlivened
Rejuvenated
Renewed
Rested
Restored
Revived

AFRAID
Apprehensive
Dread
Foreboding
Frightened
Mistrustful
Panicked

Petrified
Scared
Suspicious
Terrified
Wary
Worried

ANNOYED
Aggravated
Dismayed
Disgruntled
Displeased
Exasperated
Frustrated
Impatient
Irritated
Irked

ANGRY
Enraged
Furious
Incensed
Indignant
Irate
Livid
Outraged
Resentful

AVERSION
Animosity
Appalled
Contempt
Disgusted
Dislike
Hate
Horrified
Hostile
Repulsed

CONFUSED
Ambivalent
Baffled
Bewildered
Dazed
Hesitant
Lost
Mystified
Perplexed
Puzzled
Torn

DISCONNECTED
Alienated
Aloof
Apathetic
Bored
Cold

Detached
Distant
Distracted
Indifferent
Numb
Removed
Uninterested
Withdrawn

DISQUIET
Agitated
Alarmed
Discombobu-
    lated
Disconcerted
Disturbed
Perturbed
Rattled
Restless
Shocked
Startled
Surprised
Troubled
Turbulent
Turmoil
Uncomfortable
Uneasy
Unnerved
Unsettled
Upset

EMBARRASSED
Ashamed
Chagrined
Flustered
Guilty
Mortified
Self-Conscious

FATIGUE
Beat
Burnt Out
Depleted
Exhausted
Lethargic
Listless
Sleepy
Tired
Weary
Worn Out

PAIN
Agony
Anguished
Bereaved
Devastated

Grief
Heartbroken
Hurt
Lonely
Miserable
Regretful
Remorseful

SAD
Depressed
Dejected
Despair
Despondent
Disappointed
Discouraged
Disheartened
Forlorn
Gloomy
Heavy Hearted
Hopeless
Melancholy
Unhappy
Wretched

TENSE
Anxious
Cranky
Distressed
Distraught
Edgy
Fidgety
Frazzled
Irritable
Jittery
Nervous
Overwhelmed
Restless
Stressed Out

VULNERABLE
Fragile
Guarded
Helpless
Insecure
Leery
Reserved
Sensitive
Shaky

YEARNING
Envious
Jealous
Longing
Nostalgic
Pining
Wistful

B HOUSEHOLD CHORE INVENTORY

Make your own list of all the chores needed to run your household. Separate them into daily, weekly, monthly, seasonal, and whatever other frequency is necessary and helpful for your household. Personalize these lists to fit your household.

Next to each chore, initial who is responsible for that chore, either partner A, B, A and B, or Other. (Who will arrange for and check on "Other"?)

Housework is a cinch provided
your standards are low enough.

—Marianne Neifert, M.D.

Daily Cleaning Activities

- Prepare breakfast
- Clean up breakfast
- Prepare snacks
- Clean up snacks
- Prepare lunch
- Clean up lunch
- Prepare dinner
- Clean up dinner
- Straighten the bathrooms daily (hang towels, wipe surfaces, put things away)
- Straighten the kitchen daily (dishes, table, counter, put things away)
- Straighten the bedrooms daily (make bed, pick up clothes, put things away)
- Take out the kitchen trash (How often?)
- Straighten the entry area
- Straighten the public living area
- Straighten the public eating area
- Get the mail
- Organize the mail
- Respond to the mail (this may be weekly with some daily)
- Feed and care for pets (clean up after pets)
- Hang clean clothes
- Put dirty clothes in the laundry pile

Weekly Cleaning Activities

- Empty all the wastebaskets (How often?)
- Clean the bathrooms weekly (sink, toilet, tub, shower, floor, mirror)
- Clean the kitchen weekly or bi-weekly (counter, floor, appliances)
- Clean the bedrooms weekly (change linens, vacuum, dust, mirrors)
- Vacuum (can be broken up into segments such as by floor, and different rooms may have different frequency, public living areas may be twice a week)
- Clean mirrors and weekly window surfaces that need it (window over the kitchen sink)
- Dust and polish
- Mop floors (entry, baths, kitchen)
- Clean trim and corners if necessary
- Water indoor plants (this may be a more frequent chore)
- Water outdoor yard and plants (this may be a more frequent chore)
- Outdoor yard care (trim, mow, sweep, shovel)
- Taking the trash cans to the street and back
- Organizing the recyclables
- Taking the recyclables to the street or the recycling center

- Grocery and household list
- Grocery shopping
- Grocery organizing
- Household errands (run out of something, fix something)
- Auto care for each vehicle (gas, cleaning, maintenance, repairs)
- Garage care (organizing and cleaning)
- Personal laundry
- Household laundry
- Extra pet care (grooming, appointments, supplies, bedding, boxes)
- Clean electronics areas (wires, games, computers)
- Banking errands

Monthly Chores and Seasonal Chores

- Pay bills
- Reconcile monthly budget
- Balance checkbook
- Household repair and maintenance
- Auto repair and maintenance
- Yard maintenance
- Deep cleaning jobs
- Major organizational jobs (closets, garage, rearranging rooms)
- Good Will donations

POWER AND CONTROL WHEEL

DOMESTIC ABUSE INTERVENTION PROJECT
202 East Superior Street
Duluth, Minnesota 55802
218-722-2781
www.duluth-model.org

"It is impossible to improve a relationship if your partner believes he is entitled to have power and control over you. Partner abuse has been shown to increase in intensity and frequency unless the person who is doing the abusing chooses to seek professional help. Just as victims do not cause the abuse, survivors can not stop the abuse by simply changing their own behavior. <u>In fact, reclaiming your own power may initially put you in more danger if your partner perceives a loss of control.</u> If you think you might be in an abusive relationship, a good resource is Lundy Brancroft's book "Why Does He Do That?" I also strongly encourage you to seek information and assistance from your local domestic violence agency."

Joanna Pepin, M.S., L.M.F.T.A.

If you are here for four more years or four more weeks, you are here right now. I think when you are somewhere you ought to be there. Because it's not about how long you stay in a place, it's about what you do while you're there, and when you go, is that place any better for you having been there.

—Chris in the Morning on
Northern Exposure

Resources Referred to, Recommended, or Recognized as Influences

BOOKS, ARTICLES, PLAYS, MOVIES, TELEVISION SHOWS, WEBSITES

Books

Alberti, Robert E. and Michael L. Emmons. *Your Perfect Right: Assertiveness and Equality in Your Life and Relationships (9th Edition)*. California: Impact Publishers, 2008.

Amen, Daniel G. *Change Your Brain, Change Your Life: The Breakthrough Program for Conquering Anxiety, Depression, Obsessiveness, Anger, and Impulsiveness*. New York: Random House, 1999.

Bankcroft, Lundy. *Why Does He Do That: Inside the Minds of Angry and Controlling Men*. New York: Berkeley Books, 2003.

Bigner, Jerry, and Joseph L. Wetchler. *Relationship Therapy With Same-Sex Couples*. New York: Haworth Press, 2004.

Bloomfield, Harold, and Leonard Felder. *Making Peace with Your Parents*. New York: Ballentine, 1996.

Campbell, Joseph, and Bill Moyers. *The Power of Myth*. New York: Anchor Books, 1991.

Dalai Lama and Howard C. Cutler. *The Art of Happiness: A Handbook for Living*. New York: Penguin Books, 1998.

Dale, Ralph A. *Tao Te Ching*. New York: Barnes and Noble, 2002.

Deng, Ming-Dao. *365 Tao: Daily Meditations*. San Francisco: HarperCollins, 1992.

Dym, Barry, and Michael Glenn. *Couples: Exploring and Understanding the Cycles of Intimate Relationships*. New York: Perennial, 1994.

Fisher, Roger, William Ury, and Bruce Patton. *Getting to Yes: Negotiating Agreement Without Giving In*. New York: Penguin Books, 1991.

Fitzgerald, Edward. *Rubiat of Omar Khayyam Translated Into English Quatrains*. New York: Random House, 1947.

Forward, Susan and Craig Buck. *Toxic Parents: Overcoming Their Hurtful Legacy and Reclaiming Your Life*. New York: Bantam, 2002.

Friedman, Edwin H. *Friedman's Fables*. New York: Guilford Press, 1990.

Fromm, Eric. *The Art of Loving*. New York: Bantam, 2006.

Gibran, Kahlil. *The Prophet*. New York: Alfred A. Knopf, 1973.

Glass, Shirley P., and Jean Coppock Staeheli. *Not "Just Friends": Rebuilding Trust and Recovering Your Sanity After Infidelity*. New York: Free Press, 2004.

Goleman, Daniel. *Emotional Intelligence*. New York: Bantam, 2010.

Gottman, John M. *Why Marriages Succeed or Fail: And How You Can Make Yours Last*. New York: Simon and Schuster, 1998.

Gottman, John M. and Nan Silver. *The Seven Principles for Making Marriage Work*. New York: Three Rivers Press, 2004.

Hahn, Thich Nhat. *Peace Is Every Step: The Path of Mindfulness in Everyday Life*. Boston: Beacon Press, 1995.

Halpern, Howard M. *Cutting Loose: An Adult's Guide to Coming to Terms with Your Parents*. New York: Simon and Schuster, 2005.

Hargrave, Terry D. *The Essential Humility of Marriage: Honoring the Third Identity in Couple Therapy*. Phoenix: Zeig, Tucker and Theisen, 2000.

Hesley, John and Jan Hesley. *Rent Two Films and Let's Talk in the Morning: Using Popular Movies in Psychotherapy*. New York: Wiley and Sons, 2001.

Kabat-Zinn, Jon. *Wherever You Go, There You Are: Mindfulness Meditation In Everyday Life*. New York: Hyperion, 1994.

Kabat-Zinn, Jon, and Joan Borysenko. *Full Catastrophe Living: How to Cope with Stress, Pain, and Illness Using Mindfulness Meditation*. New York: Hyperion, 1996.

Keirsey, David, and Marilyn Bates. *Please Understand Me: Character and Temperament Types*. California: Prometheus Nemesis, 1984.

Kushner, Harold S. *When All You've Ever Wanted Isn't Enough: The Search for a Life That Matters*. New York: Random House, 2002.

———. *When Bad Things Happen to Good People*. New York: Random House, 2004.

Ladinsky, Daniel and Hafiz. *The Gift*. New York: Penguin, 1999.

Levine, Stephen. *A Year to Live: How to Live This Year as If It Were Your Last*. New York: Random House, 1998.

Lindbergh, Anne Morrow. *Gift from the Sea: 50th Anniversary Edition*, Toronto: Random House, 1991.

Louden, Jennifer. *Couple's Comfort Book: A Creative Guide for Renewing Passion, Pleasure and Commitment*. New York: Harper Collins, 2005.

———. *Woman's Comfort Book: A Self-Nurturing Guide for Restoring Balance in Your Life*. New York: Harper Collins, 2005.

Markham, Howard J., Scott M. Stanley, and Susan L. Blumberg. *Fighting for Your Marriage: Positive Steps for Preventing Divorce and Preserving a Lasting Love*. San Francisco: Wiley & Sons, Inc., 2001.

Martel, Yann. *Life of Pi*. New York: Harvest Books, 2003.

Mastin, Ric, and Billie B. Mastin. *His and Hers: A Voyage through Middle-Age Crazies*. California: Sun-Ink Presentations, 1978.

Mastin, Ric. *They Are All Gone Now*. California: Sun-Ink Presentations, 1985.

McGoldrick, Monica, and Froma Walsh. *Living Beyond Loss: Death in the Family, Second Edition*. New York: Norton, 2004.

Muller, Wayne. *Sabbath: Restoring the Sacred Rhythm of Rest*. New York: Bantam, 1999.

Olson, David H., and Amy K. Olson. *Empowering Couples Building on Your Strengths*. Minnesota: Innovations Press, 2000.

Pittman, Frank. *Man Enough: Fathers, Sons, and the Search for Masculinity*. New York: Berkley Publishing, 1994.

Powell, John Joseph. *Why Am I Afraid to Tell You Who I Am? Insights into Personal Growth*. Texas: Thomas MooreAssociation, 1995.

Riso, Don Richard, and Russ Hudson. *The Wisdom of the Enneagram: The Complete Guide to Psychological and Spiritual Growth for the Nine Personality Types*. New York: Bantam, 1999.

Robin, Viki, Joe Dominguez, and Monique Tilford. *Your Money or Your Life: 9 Steps to Transforming Your Relationship with Money and Achieving Financial Independence: Revised and Updated for the 21st Century*. New York: Penguin Books, 2008.

Rosenberg, Marshall B. *Non-Violent Communication: A Language of Life*. California: Puddle Dancer Press, 2003.

Sark. *Living Juicy: Daily Morsels for Your Creative Soul.* California: Celestial Arts, 1994.

Satir, Virginia. *The New Peoplemaking.* Palo Alto: Science and Behavior, Inc., 1988.

Scarf, Maggie. *Intimate Partners: Patterns in Love and Marriage.* New York: Ballentine, 2008.

Schnarch, David M. *Passionate Marriage: Keeping Love and Intimacy Alive in Committed Relationships.* New York: Norton, 2009.

Schwartz, Richard. *Introduction to the Internal Family Systems Model.* Oak Park: Trailheads Publication, 2001.

Tolle, Eckert. *A New Earth: Awakening to Your Life's Purpose.* New York: Penguin, 2006.

Viorst, Judith. *Necessary Losses: The Loves, Illusions, Dependencies, and Impossible Expectations That All of Us Have to Give Up in Order to Grow.* New York: Simon and Schuster, 1998.

Weiner-Davis, Michele. *Divorce Busting: A Step-by-Step Approach to Making Your Marriage Loving Again.* New York: Simon and Schuster, 1993

White, Michael, and Epston, David. *Narrative Means to Therapeutic Ends.* New York: Norton, 1990.

Wolfelt, Alan. *Understanding Your Grief: Ten Essential Touchstones for Finding Hope and Healing Your Heart.* Colorado: Companion Press, 2004.

Children's Books

Aliki. *Feelings.* New York: Greenwillow Books, 1984.

Brown, Laurie Krasny. *How to Be a Friend.* Boston: Little, Brown and Company, 1998.

Buscalia, Leo. *The Fall of Freddie the Leaf.* New Jersey: Slack, 1982.

Gackenbach, Dick. *Harry and the Terrible Whatzit.* New York: Houghton Mifflin, 1977.

Hanson, Warren. *The Next Place.* Minneapolis: Waldman House, 1997.

Huebner, Dawn. *What to Do When You Worry Too Much.* Washington, D.C.: Magination Press, 2006.

Johnson, Crockett. *Harold and the Purple Crayon.* New York: Harper Collins, 1983.

Lee, Harper. *To Kill a Mockingbird.* New York: Harper Collins, 2002

Lowery, Lois. *The Giver.* New York: Delacorte Press, 1993.

Mayer, Mercer. *There's a Nightmare in My Closet.* New York: Penguin Books, 1968.

Parnell, Peter, and Richardson, Justin. *And Tango Makes Three.* New York: Simon and Schuester, 2005.

Saint-Exupery, Antoine. *Le Petit Prince.* New York: Harvest Books, 1971.

Dr. Seuss. *And to Think that I Saw It on Mulberry Street.* New York: Random House, 1989.

———. *My Many Colored Days.* New York: Random House, 1986.

———. *Yertle the Turtle.* New York: Random House, 1979.

Silverstein, Shel. *The Giving Tree.* New York: Harper Collins, 1964.

———. *The Missing Piece.* New York: Harper Collins, 1976.

Viorst, Judith. *Alexander and the Terrible, Horrible, No Good Very Bad Day.* New York: Atheneum Books, 1972.

Plays

Becker, Rob. *Defending the Caveman*, SanFrancisco: Theatre Premier, 1991. Official website: http://www.defendingthecaveman.com

Witty, Jeff. *Avenue Q: The Musical*, New York: Theatre Premier, Director J. Moore, Music and Lyrics R. Lopez and J. Marx. Official website: http://www.avenueq.com

Articles

Haddock, S. A., and T. S. Zimmerman.2001. "The Power Equity Guide: An Activity to Assist Couples in Negotiating a Fair and Equitable Relationship." *Journal of Activities in Psychotherapy Practice 1.*

Haddock, S. A., T.S. Zimmerman, L. Current, and A. Harvey. 2002. "The Parenting Practices of Dual-Earner Couples Who Successfully Balance Family and Work." *Journal of Feminist Family Therapy 14.*

Haddock, S. A., T.S. Zimmerman, S. Ziemba, and K.P. Lyness. 2006. "Practices of Dual Earner Couples Successfully Balancing Work and Family." *Journal of Family Economic Issues* 27(2).

Lyness, K. P., S. Haddock, and T.S. Zimmerman. 2003. "Contextual Issues in Marriage and Family Therapy: Gender, Culture, and Spirituality." In *An Introduction to Marriage and Family Therapy*, edited by L. Hecker, and J. Wetchler, 409-448. Binghamton, MA: Haworth.

Zimmerman, T. S. 2000. "Marital Equality and Satisfaction in Stay-At-Home Mother and Stay-At-Home Father Families." *Contemporary Family Therapy* 22.

Zimmerman, T. S., K.E. Holm, K.C. Daniels, and S.A. Haddock. 2002. "Barriers and Bridges to Intimacy and Mutuality: A Critical Review of Sexual Advice Found in Self-Help Bestsellers." *Contemporary Family Therapy*, 24(2).

Zimmerman, T. S., S.A. Haddock, Ziemba, and A. Rust. 2002. "Family Organization Labor: Who's Calling the Plays?" *Journal of Feminist Family Therapy*, 13(2/3).

Movies

Being There. Directed by H. Ashby. Produced by A. Braunsberg. Hollywood, CA: Lorimar Film Entertainment, 1980. (Actors:Peter Sellers and Shirley MacLaine)

Chocolat. Directed by L. Hallstrom. Produced by H. Weinstein and B. Weinstein. Middlesex , England: Shepperton Studios, 2000. (Actors: Juliette Binoche, Judy Dench, and Johnny Depp)

The Doctor. Directed by R. Haines. Produced by L.Ziskin. Los Angeles, CA: Silver Screen Partners IV 1991. (Actors: William Hurt and Elizabeth Perkins)

Fearless. Directed by P. Weir. Produced by R. Yglesias. Arvin, CA: Warner Bros,1993. (Actors: Jeff Bridges, Isabella Rossellini, and Rosie Perez)

The Great Santini. Directed by L.J. Carlino. Produced by C. Pratt. Arvin. CA: Warner Bros, 1979. (Actors: Robert Duvall and Blythe Danner)

Hope Floats. Directed by F. Witaker. Produced by L. Obst and S. Bullock. Hollywood, CA: Twentieth Century Fox Film Corporation, 1998. (Actors: Sandra Bullock, Harry Connick, Jr. and Gena Rowlands.)

How to Make an American Quilt. Directed by J. Moorhouse. Produced by S. Pillsbury and M. Sanford. Banning, CA: Amblin Entertainment, 1995. (Actors: Winona Rider, Anne Bankroft, Ellen Burstyn, Kate Nelligan and Alfie Woodard.)

I Am Sam. Directed by J. Nelson. Produced by J. Nelson. Los Angeles, CA: New Line Cinema, 2001. (Actors: Sean Penn and Michelle Pfeiffer)

The Kid. Directed by J. Turteltaub. Produced by J. Turteltaub. Los Angeles, CA: Disney, 2000. (Actor: Bruce Willis)

King of Hearts. Directed by P. deBroca. Produced by P. deBroca. Senlis, France: Fidebroc,1966. (Actors: Alan Bates and Genevieve Bujold)

The Mirror Has Two Faces. Directed by B. Streisand. Produced by B. Streisand. New York City, NY: TriStar Pictures, 1996. (Actors: Barbra Streisand, Jeff Bridges, and Lauren Bacall)

Nurse Betty. Directed by N. LaBute. Produced by S. Golin. Durango, CO: Gramercy Pictures, 2000. (Actors: Renee Zellweger, Morgan Freeman, and Chris Rock)

On Golden Pond. Directed by M. Rydell. Produced by B. Gilbert. Concord, NH: IPC Films, 1981. (Actors: Katherine Hepburn, Henry Fonda, and Jane Fonda)

Regarding Henry. Directed by M. Nichols. Produced by M. Nichols. White Plains, NY: Paramount Pictures, 1991. (Actors: Harrison Ford and Annette Bening)

Wall-E. Directed by A. Stanton. Produced by J. Morris and L. Collins. USA: Pixar Animation Studios, 2008.

Television Shows

Northern Exposure. Created by J. Brand and J. Falsey. Produced by J. Brand and J. Falsey, 1990-95.

NYPD Blue. Created by S. Bochco and D. Milch. Production Company S. Bochco Productions, 1993-2005.

Websites Cited in Book

To learn more about contributors in the field of marriage and families, concepts in self-care, and online resources for humor, health, and personal growth:

American Association for Marriage and Family Therapy: http://www.AAMFT.org

Be A Good Listener: http://www.wikihow.com/Be-a-Good-Listener

Domestic Violence Intervention Project: http://www.duluth-model.org

Dulwich Centre: http:// www.dulwichcentre.com.au

Eat Right: http://www.eatright.org

The Far Side: http://www.thefarside.com

John Gottman: http://www.gottman.com

Howard Markman: http://www.loveyourrelationship.com

Mayo Clinic: http://www.mayoclinic.com/health/how-many-hours-of-sleep-are-enough

Mayo Clinic: http://www.mayoclinic.com/health/water

David Olsen: http://www.prepare-enrich.com

James O. Prochaska: http://www.prochange.com

Marshall Rosenburg: http://www.cnvc.org

David Schnarch: http://www.passionatemarriage.com

Self Leadership: http://www.selfleadership.org

TED: www.ted.com

Dr. Weil: http://www.drweil.com/drw/u/ART00521/three-breathing-exercises.html or www.stop-anxiety-attack-symptoms-com

Michele Weiner-Davis: http://www.divorcebusting.com

Bloom where you are.

Barbara Wetzel grew up in a diverse three-generation family, the oldest of four girls in Brooklyn, New York. She lives in Fort Collins, Colorado six months a year and spends the balance of her time in Cozumel, Mexico, New York City, and on the road. She and her partner of 32 years, Christopher Wells, have two adult children. Son Whitney lives in Osaka, Japan and daughter Sydney lives in Colorado.

She has a Masters Degree in Human Development and Family Studies with an emphasis in Marriage and Family Therapy from Colorado State University, and has been in private practice since 1995. She is licensed in the state of Colorado as a Marriage and Family Therapist and is a Clinical Member and an Approved Supervisor in the Association for Marriage and Family Therapists.

CPSIA information can be obtained at www.ICGtesting.com
Printed in the USA
BVOW06s1216290514

354713BV00010B/245/P